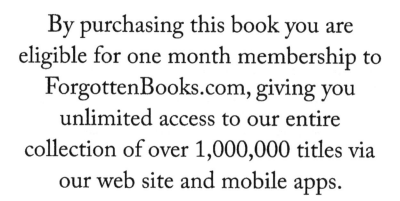

ISBN 978-0-265-85784-7
PIBN 10900254

This book is a reproduction of an important historical work. Forgotten Books uses
state-of-the-art technology to digitally reconstruct the work, preserving the original format
whilst repairing imperfections present in the aged copy. In rare cases, an imperfection in
the original, such as a blemish or missing page, may be replicated in our edition. We do,
however, repair the vast majority of imperfections successfully; any imperfections that
remain are intentionally left to preserve the state of such historical works.

MISSISSIPPI
AW JOURNAL

MAY, 1933

Published by

NIVERSITY OF MISSISSIPPI LAW SCHOOL
and
MISSISSIPPI STATE BAR

LEADING ARTICLES

COMPLETE TABLE OF CONTENTS OF THIS ISSUE
ON PAGE III

ffice at University, Mississippi, with additional
at Jackson, Tennessee.

MISSISSIPPI LAW JOURNAL

CONTENTS

MISSISSIPPI LAW JOURNAL

JOURNAL of the MISSISSIPPI STATE BAR

Vol. V	MAY, 1933	No. 3

INSTRUCTIONS TO JURIES—THEIR ROLE IN THE JUDICIAL PROCESS

(Printed by permission from YALE LAW JOURNAL.)

By R. J. FARLEY*

In the standard works on instructions to juries one is confronted by a mass of descriptive. classes of instructions. There is usually a division into definitions and distinctions, province of the court and jury, abstract and concrete statement, confinement to pleadings and evidence, presumptions and inferences, resolution of issues, commenting on the weight of evidence and cautionary instructions. The casebooks either omit the matter entirely or often give so highly strained and inadequate a treatment as to be misleading. At first glance such a method as above outlined seems quite unsatisfactory but as one progresses in analysis the more difficult it becomes to devise an improvement.

Significant is a paragraph in the publisher's preface to one of the late works on the subject:

"The supervising editor, for more than a generation has constantly watched the stream of current decisions which has flowed into the reservoir of reported cases; he has observed the questions debated and decided in these cases; and one thing that has been borne in upon him is the fact that almost one-half of the legal warfare inscribed on the pages in these opinions deals with the subject of Province of the Court and Jury, and the delimitation of that province in the instructions of the trial judge in the court below. In this stream of opinions he has seen the same case come several times before the same appellate court, indicating tragic consequences in the administration of justice, due wholly to the failure of the trial judge to instruct the jury according to the established law."[1]

* Professor of Law, University of Mississippi. This paper was written in connection with a seminar on Law Administration while the writer was a Sterling Research Fellow in the Yale School of Law. Acknowledgment is made to Professor Thurman W. Arnold of the Yale School of Law for many helpful suggestions.

[1] RANDALL, INSTRUTIONS TO JURIES (1922)iii.

No one who has observed the prevalence of cases involving instructions will question these observations, though he may wonder just what is an instruction "according to the established law." It is submitted that it is practically impossible to write an instruction of any consequence as such that could not be subjected to valid criticism as eroueous under the "established law." Similarly it is impossible to correlate the various artificialities of definition and description into a satisfactory body of doctrine. Therefore the object of a paper on instructions may well be to consider their limitations and the art and artifices in the use of them which tend to make such a correlation impossible.

An adequate presentation of the subject requires an examination of the growth of these functions. This will necessitate a sketch of the development of the jury from the standpoint of the use of the attaint and fine as early methods of control and their eventual displacement by the more effective procedure of granting new trials.[2]

Following this historial predicate, the subject will then be divided into:

I.   The Theoretical Function of Instructions to Enlighten the Jury on the Law.

II. The Function of Instructions as a Method by which Appellate Courts Control Juries and Trial Courts.

III. The Function of Instructions from the Lawyer's View-Point as Traps for the Courts.

IV. The Function of Instructions as a Method by Which the Trial Court Maintains Its Integrity.

V.   Procedural Problems Arising as a Result and the Escapes from These Problems.

Historical Introduction

The origin of a trial by jury is unknown to the authorities.[3] It is certain, however, that by the time of Henry III in criminal cases it had all the essential features known to us except that the same body sometimes discharged the functions of both a grand and petit jury.[4] And by the time

---

2 The authorities drawn on most extensively are FORSYTH, HISTORY OF TRIAL BY JURY (1852); Thayer's series of articles in (1891-92) 5 HARV. L. REV. (the material here utilized is also found in his PRELIMINARY TREATISE ON EVIDENCE (1899) BIGELOW, HISTORY OF PROCEDURE IN ENGLAND (1880); and Appendix II of Quincy's Reports (Massachusetts 1761).

3 The Statute of 13 EDW. I, c. 30 (1285) had enacted that the justices of assise should also hold inquests of trespass and other pleas wherein small examination was required and even of more important matters requiring great examination, if both parties desired it.

4 FORSYTH, op. cit. supra note 2, at 200. Even this separation had occurred by the time of Edward III. Id. at 206.

of Henry VI the requirement of personal knowledge on the part of the jurors was the only substantial dissimilarity to the modern jury in civil cases.[5]

That juries were originally bodies of witnesses, probably furnished the dominant factor in attitude for several hundred years. The more or less arbitrary control of them by the judge in earlier days[6] was as much a matter of course as is today the directing of witnesses to retire to the proper room after being sworn. There could have been no sharp cleavage between law and fact in a country where the testimony consisted of legal conclusions and God was the ruling principle.[7] As yet no importance was attached to the separation of principle from evidence or to the invasion of respective provinces.[8] If the jury took upon themselves the peril of a general verdict,[9] the recourse for dissatisfaction in civil cases was to be found in the attaint, wherein a contrary holding by a second jury of twenty-four was proof of the untruth of the first verdict and of the perjury of the twelve who had rendered it.

The use of the attaint while known as early as the

---

5 FORSYTH, *op. cit. supra* note 2, at 159, quoting FORTESCUE, DE LAUDIBUS LEGUM ANGLIAE.

6 If doubt was entertained by the judge on the verdict, he interrogated the jurors, and if he suspected them of concealing the truth examined them separately. FORSYTH, *op. cit. supra* note 2, at 206, 207. In civil cases he might re-summon them for further questioning. Brac. N. B. II, Case 887 (1232); *Id.* III, case 1226 (1237).

7 "You shall tell us by the oath which you have made whether B be fully tenant of 14 acres or not. . . . The assise came and said that B was tenant of 14 acres and that such an one was tenant of the remaining acre of the fifteen acres." Y. B. Trin. 20 Edw. I, f. 2 (1291). "N, who is here present accused of such and such a felony comes and denies it wholly, and puts himself upon your tongues concerning this for good and evil; and therefore we charge you by the faith ye owe to God, and by the oath which you have taken, that ye make us to know the truth thereon, and omit not for fear or love or hate, but having only (the fear of) God before your eyes . . .", etc. FORSYTH, *op cit. supra* note 2, at 206, 207.

8 "The twelve knights may either say, directly and shortly, that one party or the other has the greater right, or merely set forth the facts and thus enable the justices to say it—what we call a special verdict." Thayer, *The Jury and Its Development* (1892) 5 HARV. L. REV. 249, 261.

"'While the juror's oath,' said Bracton, 'has in it three associated things (*comites*) truth, justice and judgment, it is truth that is to be found in the juror, *justitia et judicium* in the judge. But sometimes judgment seems to belong to jurors since they are to say on their oath, yet according to their belief, whether so and so disseised so and so, or not.'" THAYER, PRELIMINARY TREATISE ON EVIDENCE (1898) 195, citing Bracton, f. 186 b.

9 WESTMINSTER II (13 EDW. I) c. 30 (1285) (from Statutes at Large, Owen Ruffhead, 1763) "II, . . . (4) And also it is ordained, That the Justices assigned to take Assises shall not compel the jurors to say precisely whether it be Disseisin, or not, so that they shew the Truth of the Deed, and require aid of the Justices. (5) But if they of their own Head will say, that it is Disseisin, their verdict shall be admitted at their own Peril."

eleventh century,[10] seems not to have extended to all actions in the thirteenth.[11] Its application was gradually enlarged by successive statutes,[12] until in 1360 it was finally provided "that every man against whom they [the jurors] shall pass may have the attaint both in pleas real and personal, even those too poor to pay a fee for it."[13]   But the prevalence of "perjured" verdicts continued despite all statutes. It was felt that the juries were primarily at fault, not the directions of the judges,[14] although there were occasions when the judges also were taken to task.[15] As the law progressed in refinement, the judges, chafed no doubt by the realization of their superiority as experts, began using the threat of the attaint to affright the juries into rendering special verdicts. Attaint as a method of control was not entirely effective, however, because the gentlemen preferred to pay a mean fine rather than meet to slander and deface the honest yeomen, their neighbours.[16] Its utility gradually declined although measures were passed from time to time in the hope that by making the punishment less rigorous, the attainting jury would be encouraged to meet and chasten the "honest yeomen."[17]

In criminal cases the fine seems not to have functioned much better than the attaint. There are a number of instances[18] where the jury was fined for going against the direction of the court "but these doings were even then accounted very violent, tyrannical and contrary to the liberty and custom of the realm of England." And often the juries were not afraid to "take the bit in mouth and go head-strong against the Court," much to the disgust and fury of some of the judges.[19]

In 1670 came Vaughan's memorable decision in *Bushel's*

---

10 Gundulf v. Pichot (Big. Pl. A. N.) 34 (1879) cited and summarized by Thayer, *The Jury and Its Development*, *supra* note 8, at 253; also summarized and discussed in FORSYTH, *op. cit. supra* note 3, at 100 *et seq.*

11 Y. B. Trin. 20 Edw. I, f. 18 (1291). "Note, after the Great Assise an Attaint never lies." See also Brac. N. B. II, case 350 (1229).

12 WESTMINSTER I (3 Edw. I) c. 38 (1274); 5 EDW. III, c. 7 (1331); 28 EDW. III, c. 8 (1354). See also 3 BL. COMM. *403, 404.

13 34 EDW. III, c. 7 (1360).

14 11 HEN. VI, c. 4 (1433); 15 HEN. VI, c. 5 (1436).

15 Brac. N. B. II, case 564 (1231); Brac. N. B. III, case 1166 (1235); 3 BL. COMM. *409.

16 Com. of England, Book III, c. 2; 3 Blackstone, *404, Bright v. Eynon, 1 Burr. 390 (Mansfield, 1757).

17 11 HEN. VII,.c. 21 (1495); 11 HEN. VII, c. 24 (1495); 23 HEN. VIII, c. 3 (1531); 13 ELIZ. c. 25 (1571).

18 1 How. St. Tr. 862, 869 (1554); T. Raymond 98 (K. B. 1664); Hardres 409 (Ex. 1665); Kelyng 50 (K. B. 1666); 2 Keble 180 (K. B. 1667); 6 How. St. Tr. 951 (1670) (Penn & Mead's case).

19 1 Keble 864 (K. B. 1665).

Case and in 1688 came the Revolution. Just how far this decision is a reflection of the then current thought is a matter for conjecture. Certain it is that for the next two centuries more and more dependence was placed on the jury. Heretofore, since it was necessary to trust either court or jury, there had been practically no question of the proper supremacy of the court. That there should be a specific remedy as a matter of right for the invasion of the "province" of the jury was practically unheard of.[20] The question had been viewed wholly from the perspective of the propriety of special verdicts as a means of giving the judges some voice in the application of the law. "The precedents run all for trust on the side of the court." But now the respective provinces had to be determined since this revolutionary decision had entirely splintered both principal clubs which the judges had been wont to wield as threats to the jury, the attaint and the fine.

In the course of his opinion Vaughan examined the maxim[21] that questions of law are for the court and questions of fact for the jury. It might be well to pause and briefly to trace the origin of this concept. So far as this writer can ascertain, the first clear enunciation of the principle was made by Plowden in his report of Townsend's Case wherein he comments "For the office of 12 men is no other than to inquire of Matters of Fact and not to adjudge what the Law is, for that is the Office of the Court and not of the jury. . . ."[22] And although the same idea was voiced by other writers of that and the immediately succeeding period,[23] it remained for Coke to turn it into that neat phraseology, the magic of which has captivated lawyers and judges from that day to this. It may be found in his report of Heydon's Case,[24] Altham's Case,[25] Dowman's Case,[26] Abbott of Strata Mercella's Case,[27] Priddle and Napper's Case,[28] in his commentary on Littleton,[29] and

---

20 Since the Statute of WESTMINSTER II (13 Edw. I) c. 31. (1285), there had been provision for excepting to the judge's direction which on rare occasions had been availed of but never as being an invasion of the province of the jury. See also 3 COKE, LAW OF ENGLAND *1556 (Thomas ed. 1836, p. 365, n. 7) (Hargrave's ed. 1794, *1556, n. 5).

21 Vaughan 135, 149 (C. P. 1670).

22 I Plowden 110a, 114a (K. B. 1554).

23 Hobart 53 (K. B. 1615); Dyer 362a 15 (K. B. 1557); Moore 105 (K. B. 1575); Hard. 16 (Ex. 1655); 2 Bulst. 314 (K. B. 1614).

24 2 Co. Rep., pt. 4, 41a, 42b (K. B. 1585).

25 4 Co. Rep., pt. 8, 150b (K. B. 1610).

26 5 Co. Rep., pt. 9, 7b, 13a (K. B. 1585).

27 5 Co. Rep., pt. 9, 23b, 25a (K. B. 1591).

28 6 Co. Rep., pt. 11, 8b, 10b (K. B. 1612).

29 Co. LITT. *228b (2 Hargreave's ed. 1794).

in his Law of England.[30]   But even though Coke had stated it repeatedly, Vaughan was not ready to accept it as an abstract principle of functional delimitation. Since the jury often had knowledge of facts not brought out in court, he thought it obvious that they were best fitted to decide them. But even though he recognized that the jury was incapable of deciding the law, he nevertheless insisted that whenever a verdict was returned upon general issues "they resolve the law and the fact complicately."[31]

After the Revolution the fight for the ascendancy of the jury's power continued.   Then indeed did it become the bulwark of liberty and the palladium of the rights of freemen in the war with tyrannical judges.   Eventually the fight crystallized around trials for libel,[32] and the great Mansfield, in upholding his directions to juries, became involved in the attack led by Camden, Erskine and Fox, and was made a target of "that common slanderer Junius".[33] The Society for Constitutional Information published and distributed its tract for the information of juries on their "rights under the constitution".[34]   The pot was boiling. The House of Lords submitted the questions which had arisen as to libels to all the judges and after they had reported a view substantially in accord with that theretofore announced by Lord Mansfield, the Fox Libel Bill was tardily passed in 1792.[35]   In the meantime the United States of America had come into being and the provinces of judge and jury were there also in process of delimitation.   But before turning to this country, another development in English law should be noted—that of granting new trials.

Blackstone says, "The exertion of these superintendent powers of the king's courts, in setting aside the verdict of a jury and granting a new trial, on account of misbehavior in the jurors, is of a date extremely ancient.   There are instances in the Year-Books of the reigns of Edward III, Henry IV, and Henry VII of judgments being stayed (even

---

30 *155b (3 Thomas ed. (1836) p. 365).

31 *Supra* note 21, at 149, 150.

32 Seven Bishop's case, 12 How. St. Tr. 183 (1688); Bayard's case, 14 How. St. Tr. 471, 502 (1702); Fuller's case, 14 *id.* 517 (1702); Tutchin's case, 14 *id.* 1095 (1704); Francklin's case, 17 *id.* 625 (1731); Owen's case, 18 *id.* 1203 (1752); Almon's case, 20 *id.* 803 (1770); Miller's case, 20 *id.* 869 (1770); Woodfall's case, 20 *id.* 895 (1770); Dean of St. Asaph's case, 21 *id.* 847 (1784).   See note in 8 How. St. Tr. 35 (1860).

33 For a full discussion of Lord Mansfield's part see FORSYTH. *op. cit. supra* note 2, c. XII.

34 Copy set out in full in account of Dean of St. Asaph's case, *supra* note 32, at 850.   This was the case in which the famous Erskine distinguished himself as the champion of liberty.

35 32 GEO. III, c. 60 (1791).

after a trial at bar) and new *venires* awarded, because the jury had eat and drank without consent of the judge, and because the plaintiff had privately given a paper to a jury-man before he was sworn. And upon these the chief justice Glynn, in 1655, grounded the first precedent that is reported in our books for granting a new trial upon account of *excessive damages* given by the jury.''[36]

In this first precedent,[37] the actual ground for granting the new trial is significant. ''If the court do believe that the jury gave a verdict against their direction, they may grant a new trial.'' The particular in which the jury had gone against direction was in giving excessive damages; yet in the earlier days it had not been thought necessary to have a new trial for excessive damages, the damages being summarily moderated at the discretion of the judge without regard to the jury's verdict. But that was done to avoid and to relieve from possible attaint of the jury,[38] and the attaint was now in desuetude.

After *Bushel's Case,* the new trial became more and more popular although it took some time to realize its possibilities in connection with instructions as a method of control. But after the agitation of the succeeding century on the right of the jury to decide the law, its potentialities were fully sounded. The common law courts were at first somewhat reluctant, but besides Vaughan's decision and the general heresy of jurors there was the arrogative Chancery to be considered:[39] ''Juries are wilful enough and denying a new trial here will but send parties into the Chancery.''[40]

Coeval with the granting of new trials on the ground of failure to observe the directions of the court was the development of complete separation of witness and jury,[41] a necessity more pronounced after Vaughan's decision which still acknowledged the possibility of the jury having information not otherwise known to the court.

By 1773 the practice of granting new trials on account of misdirection by the court or the jury's failure to follow

---

36 3 BL. COMM. *387, 388, citing the instance in the Year Books: 24 EDW. III, 24 (Trin. 1359); 11 HEN. IV, 18 (Mich. 1409); 14 HEN. VII, 1 (Mich. 1498).

37 Wood v. Gunston, Style 462 (K. B. 1655).

38 Bracton IV, tr. 1, c. 19, Sec. 8 and Bracton IV, tr. 5, c. 4. Cited in 3 BL. COMM. *389.

39 3 BL. COMM. *388.

40 Martyn and Jackson, 3 Keble 398 (K. B. 1674). ''Twisden and Wild refused to grant it, the jury being judges of the fact, though verdict be against the evidence, it is not to be set aside without a new law'' but Rainsford, C. J., favored granting a new trial on account of the Chancery.

41 Style 253 (K. B. 1650), 2 Salk 405 (K. B. 1702).

its directions, seems to have been well established and encouraged. We find Lord Chief Justice DeGrey prefacing an opinion with:

"I have always considered this mode of application for a new trial as very satisfactory to the suitors, who may be injured by mistake; and likewise to the jury, as it reforms their errors, if they commit any and is a happy substitute for the much more grievous proceeding that the common law directed. . . . It is possible that in many instances that mistake may arise from the direction of the Court; for the Court may direct the jury to attend to a circumstance that in point of law is not proved, or is not the subject-matter for their consideration; or it is possible that the jury may mistake the evidence as to believe the fact to be true, when it is not so; then it comes to be a proper motion for a new trial, because the verdict is contrary to the evidence."[42]

Developments in America proceeded along the same general lines. Appendix II of Quincy's Reports (Massachusetts) concludes:

"It is worthy of notice how the history of this question [the powers and rights of juries] after the English Revolution of 1688 repeated itself in America nearly a century later. The great constitutional lawyers and judges of either Revolutionary period—Somers and Holt; Adams, Jay, Wilson, Iredell, Chase, Marshall, Hamilton, Parsons and Kent—with one voice maintained the right of the jury upon the general issue to judge of the law as well as the fact. But they had hardly passed away, or fifty years elapsed since either Revolution, when the courts of the new government began to assert as much control over the consciences of the jury, as had been claimed by the most arbitrary judges of the Monarch whom that Revolution had overthrown."[43]

The rights and powers of juries were tested in libels in colonial America as well as in England. The trial of John Peter Zenger, printer, before Hon. James de Lancey, Esq., Chief Justice of the Province of New York in 1735, "made a great noise in the world," and one Mr. Hamilton, a Philadelphia lawyer, successfully argued both law and fact to the jury despite the protest of the Chief Justice.

John Adams did not fare so well as counsel in a civil action for libel in 1767 when he attempted to argue to the jury whether the words were actionable or not. Justices Lynde, Cushing, Oliver and Trowbridge, of the Massachusetts Bay Province, would not permit it. But in the *Trial of the British Soldiers,* although the same Justice Trowbridge instructed the jury that they were to take the law from the Court, John Adams nevertheless argued the law at

---

42 Fabrigas v. Mostyn, 20 How. St. Tr. 82, 175 (1773).
43 Quincy, *op. cit. supra* note 2, at 559.

length to the jury and continued thereafter in the opinion that juries may. decide the law even in civil cases notwithstanding the instructions of the court.

In America by the time of the Revolution and for some time thereafter, the power to decide the law in criminal cases seems to have been almost universally accorded the jury and quite generally, it determined the law in civil cases.[44]   Chief Justice Jay in 1794 in a civil cause "regarded as of first importance," instructed the jury on "the good old rule, that on questions of fact, it is the province of the jury, on questions of law, it is the province of the court to decide.   But it must be observed that by the same law, which recognizes this reasonable distribution of jurisdiction, you have nevertheless a right to take upon yourselves to judge of both, and to determine the law as well as the fact in controversy.   On this and on every other occasion, however, we have no doubt, you will pay that respect, which is due to the opinion of the court: For, as on the one hand, it is presumed that juries are the best judges of facts; it is, on the other hand, presumable that the court are the best judges of the law.   But still both objects are lawfully within your power of decision."[45]

And in the next year Justice Iredell digressed to remark that even though instructed by the court to find for the defendant, much as they may respect the sentiments of the court on points of law, "they are not bound to deliver a verdict conformably to them."[46]

Already some one had conceived the utility of distinguishing between *power* and *right* but Justice James Kent smashed it such a blow that it did not show signs of recovery in New York for some years.   He found it impossible to meet the stream of authority that the jury can make up a verdict of fact and law against all direction of the judge. And as for denying that they can rightfully and lawfully exercise such a power without "compromitting their consciences," the law must

"have intended in granting this power to a jury, to grant them a lawful and rightful power, or it would have provided a remedy against the undue exercise of it.   The true criterion of a legal power, is its capacity to produce a definitive effect liable neither to censure nor review.   And the verdict of not guilty, in a criminal case, is, in every respect absolutely final.   The jury are not liable to punishment, nor the verdict to control.   No attaint lies, nor can a new trial be awarded.   The exercise of this power in

---

44 For a full discussion see Quincy *op. cit. supra* note 2, at 567 *et seq.*
45 Georgia v. Brailsford, 3 Dall. 1, 4 (1794).
46 Bingham v. Cabbot, 3 Dall. 19, 33 (1795).

the jury has been sanctioned, and upheld in constant activity, from the earliest ages.''[47]

He admitted however that in civil cases, the opinion of the court on questions of law ought ultimately to be enforced by the power of setting aside the verdict and granting new trials.[48]

There is small room for doubt that the jury reached its zenith before 1835, when Justice Story, as circuit judge, instructing a jury, made a point upon which he had had a decided opinion during his whole professional life. He said that regardless of physical *power* and the necessity of compounding law and fact, the jury had no *moral right* to decide the law according to their own notions. On the contrary, he held it the most sacred constitutional right of every party accused of crime that the jury should respond as to the facts and the court as to the law. Indeed, he said that if he had thought otherwise, he would abstain from instructing them on the law at all.[49]

The heyday of the appellate courts had arrived. The reversal of the lower courts and the granting of new trials had become a common-place. The fear of judges had passed.[50] But the jury proponents did not surrender without a struggle. In Massachusetts, Pennsylvania, and New York, the contest was particularly prolonged.[51] Vermont, too, attempted to stem the tide.[52]

It would be interesting and no doubt possible to correlate to an unusual degree the rise and fall of the notion of the necessity of jury supremacy with the advance and recession of the frontier in its progress through the various states. The last frontier faded out in the nineties and it is significant perhaps that during that decade the question was finally refined and resolved into its present status.

---

47 People v. Croswell, 3 John. Cas. *337, *356 (N. Y. 1804).

48 *Id.* at *376.

49 U. S. v. Battiste, Fed. Cas. No. 14545 (1835).

50 Williams v. State, 32 Miss. 389, 396 (1856); see Sparf v. United States, 156 U. S. 51, 90 (1895).

51 Massachusetts: Coffin v. Coffin, 4 Mass. 1, 25 (1808) Commonwealth v. Blanding, 3 Pick. 304 (1825); Commonwealth v. Knapp, 10 Pick. 477, 496 (1830); Commonwealth v. Kneeland, 20 Pick. 206, 227 (1838); Commonwealth v. Porter, 10 Metc. 263 (1845); Commonwealth v. Martin, 5 Gray 303, note (1855); Commonwealth v. Rock, 10 Gray 4 (1857); New York: People v Croswell, *supra* note 47; People v. Thayer, 1 Parker C. C. 595 (1825); People v. Videto, *id.* 603 (1825); People v. Pine, 2 Barb. 566 (1848); Carpenter v. People, 8 Barb. 603, 611 (1850); Pennsylvania: Albertson's Lessee v. Robeson, 1 Dall. 9 (1764); Wilcox v. Henry, 1 Dall. 69, 71 (1782); Pennsylvania v. Bell, Addison R. 156, 160, 161 (1793); Guffy v. Commonwealth, 2 Grant 66, 68 (1853).

52 See the majority and dissenting opinions in State v. Croteau, 23 Vt. 14 (1849).

During that period there stand out three compelling decisions in the cases of *Commonwealth v. McManus*,[53] *State v. Burpee*,[54] and *Sparf et al. v. United States*,[55] in each of which there was dissent.

While the provinces of court and jury were being defined by the judiciary, the legislatures had not been inactive. Among other problems which had received the attention of the latter, was the need of accurately recording just what the judges had stated the law to be so that appellate courts might know certainly[56] whether the juries had failed to follow it. Under the common law, instructions were oral[57] and before the statutory change it was incumbent upon the person excepting to get them reduced to writing, for recordation was discretionary with the trial judge.[58]

The requirement that instructions be written,[59] innocent enough in its avowed objective, has furnished one of the most effective devices for the supremacy of appellate courts, not only in the control of the jury but of the trial court as well. By means of interpretative rules as to the

---

53 143 Pa. 64, 21 Atl. 1018, 22 Atl. 761 (1891).

54 65 Vt. 1, 25 Atl. 964 (1892).

55 *Supra* note 50.

56 People v. Hersey, 53 Cal. 574 (1879).

57 See Vicksburg Rr. Co. v. Putnam, 118 U. S. 545 (1886). ''In the courts of the United States, as in those of England, from which our practice was derived, the judge, in submitting a case to a jury, may at his discretion, whenever he thinks fit to assist them in arriving at a just conclusion, comment upon the evidence, call their attention to parts of it which he thinks important, and express his opinion on the facts . . .''

58 Smith v. Crichton, 33 Md. 103 (1870).

59 Ala. Code (Michie, 1928) Sec. 9508; Ariz. Code (Struckmeyer, 1928) Secs. 3809, 3810; Ark. Const. of 1874 Art. VII. Sec. 23; Cal. Pen. Code (Deering, 1931) Sec. 1127c; and Cal. Code Civ. Proc. (Deering, 1931) Sec. 608; Colo. Ann. Stat. (Mills, 1930) Secs. 2214, 2215; Fla. Comp. Laws (1927) Secs. 4364, 4365; Ga. Code (Michie, 1926) Sec. 4847; Idaho Comp. Stat. (1919) Sec. 6847; Ill. Rev. Stat. (Smith-Hurd, 1931) c. 110, Sec. 73; Ind. Ann. Stat. (Burn's, 1926) Sec. 584, cl. 5; Iowa Code (1931) Secs. 11491, 11506; Kan. Rev. Stat. Ann. (1923) Sec. 60-2909 cl. 5; Ky. Code Ann. (Carroll, 1927) Civ. Prac. Sec. 317, cl. 5, Crim. Prac. Sec. 225; La. Code of Practice (Dart, 1932) art. 515; Me. Rev. Stat. (1930) c. 96, Sec. 104; Miss. Code Ann. (1930) Sec. 586; Mo. Rev. Stat. (1929) Civ. Sec. 967, Crim. Sec. 3694; Mont. Rev. Code (1921) Civ. Sec. 9349, Pen. Sec. 11969; Neb. Comp. Stat. (1929) Secs. 20-1107, 20-1111, 29-2016; N. M. Stat. Ann. (Courtright, 1929) Secs. 70-104, 70-108; N. C. Code (1931) Sec. 566; Ohio Gen. Code (Page, 1926) Sec. 11447; N. D. Comp. Laws Ann. (1913) Secs. 7620, 10822; Ore. Code Ann. (1930) Sec. 2-301, cl. 6; Tenn. Code (1932) Civ. Secs. 8809, 8810, Crim. Secs. 11749, 11750; Tex. Ann. Civ. & Crim. Stat. (Vernon, 1925) Civ. Secs. 2184, 2185, Crim. Secs. 658, 659, 663; Utah Comp. Laws (1917) Civ. Sec. 6802, Crim. Sec. 8975; Wash. Comp. Stat. (Remington, 1922) Secs. 339, 2158; W. Va. Code (1931) c. 56, art. 6, Sec. 19; Wis. Stat. (1931) Secs. 270-271; Wyo. Rev. Stat. (1931) Civ. Sec. 89-1306, cl. 6, Crim. Sec. 33-902, cl. 6. (While a number of these statutes make written instructions mandatory, others provide that they shall be reduced to writing upon request of either party.)

giving and refusing of instructions, and the form and necessity of written instructions, many of the attempted lines of cleavage between law and fact and the provinces of court and jury, have been drawn. Since the court's province was the law, it was quite logically provided in the majority of the states either by statute, judicial decisions or constitutional enactment that in giving the instructions, the court should not charge the jury with respect to the facts or the weight to be accorded them.[60]

At last this troublesome phase of administration had been co-ordinated, articulated and perfected—or so it may have been thought. Each branch of the administration now had seemingly a well-defined province of activity.

I

The Theoretical Function of Instructions to Enlighten the Jury on the Law

On the theory that at the end of a hearing the court is cognizant of the legal issues in question, and the jury is in full possession of the relevant facts, nothing would seem more simple than for the court to announce the law appropriate to the occasion and for the jury thereupon to reach a just verdict by applying it. This is the theory of instructions. Their avowed function is to state the substantive law as a text-book for the jury against a background of the individual case, with due care not to make it

---

60 Daniel v. Wade, 203 Ala. 335, 83 So. 99 (1919); Southern Pacific Rr. v. Hogan, 13 Ariz. 34, 108 Pac. 240 (1910); Free v. Maxwell, 138 Ark. 489, 212 S. W. 325 (1919); McNeil v. Barney, 51 Cal. 603 (1877) (See also CAL. CONST. art. VI, Sec. 19); Farnsworth v. Tampa Electric Co., 62 Fla. 166, 57 So. 233 (1911); Owen v. Palmour, 111 Ga. 885, 36 S. E. 969 (1900); Jennings v. Baltimore & Ohio Rr. Co., 195 Ill. App. 543 (1915); Virgin v. Lake Erie & Western Rr. Co., 55 Ind. App. 216, 101 N. E. 500 (1913); Carroll v. Chicago, St. Paul Rr. Co., 103 Iowa 134, 84 N. W. 1035 (1901); Ennis-Bayard Petroleum Co. v. Mill & Elevator Co., 118 Kan. 202, 235 Pac. 119 (1925); Louisiana & Northern Rr. Co. v. Lynch, 137 Ky. 696, 126 S. W. 362 (1910); State v. King, 135 La. 117, 64 So. 1007 (1914); Hayden v. Me. Central Rr. Co., 118 Me. 442, 108 Atl. 681 (1920); Western Md. Rr. Co. v. Shivers, 101 Md. 391, 61 Atl. 618 (1905); Davis v. Jenney, 42 Mass. 221 (1840); Kearney v. State, 68 Miss. 233, 8 So. 292 (1890); Winter v. Supreme Lodge Knights of Pythias, 96 Mo. App. 1, 69 S. W. 662 (1902); State v. Mahoney, 24 Mont. 281, 61 Pac. 647 (1900); Hanika v. Lincoln Trac. Co., 98 Neb. 583, 153 N. W. 568 (1915); Victor American Fuel Co. v. Melkusch, 24 N. M. 47, 173 Pac. 198 (1918); Ray v. Patterson, 170 N. C. 226, 87 S. E. 212 (1915); Commercial Security Co. v. Jolly, 103 Okla. 8, 229 Pac. 193 (1924); State v. McAllister, 67 Ore. 480, 136 Pac. 354 (1913); Moore v. Cummings, 87 S. C. 166, 69 S. E. 154 (1910); Fellows v. Christensen, 28 S. D. 353, 133 N. W. 814 (1911); Earp v. Edington, 107 Tenn. 23, 64 S. W. 40 (1901); Kansas City Rr. Co. v. Corn, 186 S. W. 807 (Tex. Civ. App. 1916); Schuyler v. Southern Pacific Rr. Co., 37 Utah 581, 109 Pac. 458 (1910); Gunter v. Hughes, 143 Va. 36, 129 S. E. 239 (1925); State v. Greer, 22 W. Va. 800 (1883); Hempton v. State, 111 Wis. 127, 86 N. W. 596 (1901), and see WIS. CONST. art. 5, sec. 26.

abstract and at the same time not to be so particular as to trench on the facts. That this of course is practically a physical impossibility, is easily apprehended. Consequently, the trial judge undertakes to give an exposition of the principles of law appropriate to the case,[61] restricted to the matters in issue,[62] in such manner as to be readily understood by the mind untrained in the law.[63] The issues must be presented in the most intelligible form,[64] and the principles of evidence suggested wherever necessary.[65] The sum total must be addressed to the facts to be found by the jury,[66] in order to enable them better to understand their duty and to prevent them from arriving at wrong conclusions. But nevertheless care must be taken not to overstep the *plain* boundary that separates the provinces of court and jury.[67]

Taking some such operating theorem as the foregoing, the standard works treating of instructions proceed to reduce it to its logical heads and sub-heads. But regardless of the particular choice of topical analysis, it will be readily seen from a perusal of the cases that, except for the matter based on necessity for written instructions and the procedure in excepting, the crux of instructional administration lies in the constant attempt at description of the elusive lines of demarcation between law and fact, the duty of the court to give the law applicable to the particular case without invading the province of the jury, and the duty of the jury to receive that law and obediently apply it to the proper facts. And to make bad matters worse there is the apparent occasional compromise when the court may submit so-called mixed questions of law and fact to the jury under proper instruction.[68]

After a reading of the ordinary materials on instructions

---

61 Lehman v. Hawks, 121 Ind. 541, 23 N. E. 670 (1889); Terry v. Davenport, 170 Ind. 74, 83 N. E. 636 (1908).

62 St. Louis, Iron Mountain & Southern Ry. Co. v. Thurman, 110 Ark. 188, 161 S. W. 1054 (1913).

63 Pagels v. Meyer, 193 Ill. 172, 61 N. E. 1111 (1901).

64 Owen v. Owen, 22 Iowa 270 (1867); Louisiana & Northern Rr. Co. v. King's Adm'r., 131 Ky. 347, 115 S. W. 196 (1909).

65 Souvais v. Leavitt, 50 Mich. 108, 15 N. W. 37 (1883); Welch v. Ware, 32 Mich. 77 (1875).

66 Hanson v. Kent & Purdy Co., 36 Okla. 583, 129 Pac. 7 (1912); Rio Grande Southern Rr. Co. v. Campbell, 44 Colo. 1, 96 Pac. 986 (1908).

67 Gillett v. Webb, 17 Ill. App. 458 (1885).

68 For example: "The submission of the question [proximate cause] to the sound discretion of the jury, under proper instructions, was a disposition of the case in harmony with the long line of authorities cited by counsel on both sides." Chester Nat'l Bank v. Southern Pipe Line Co., 40 Pa. Sup. Ct. 87, 96 (1909). This is probably of most common occurrence today in negligence cases.

one is impressed with the distinct hazard of asking for any instructions whatsoever. Of course the great variety of procedure in obtaining instructions—varying from the rule in Mississippi,[69] where the court is forbidden to give any instructions not asked for, to the practice in the federal courts, where the court is allowed the utmost leeway—tends to accentuate the confusion and to make difficult a general treatment of the rules. But aside from this, the refinement of the larger principles themselves appear to be such as to make an instruction that escapes Scylla fall directly into Charybdis: For an example, take one principle—the relation of the pleadings and evidence.

In general, the instructions must be within the purview of the pleadings and predicated thereupon.[70] They must be neither broader nor narrower than the pleadings nor suggestive of issues not raised thereby.[71] These issues must be restricted further to those raised and supported by the evidence,[72] and care must be exercised not to assume the existence or non-existence of any facts.[73] Yet there must be no omission or exclusion of any issues, theories, or defenses, even though the evidence is very slight.[74] And the whole must be so balanced as neither to give undue prominence to particular evidence, theories or issues,[75] nor to call specific attention to the claims of one without adverting to the corresponding claims of the other party.[76]

When one considers the apparent nicety required in framing an instruction that will conform to the above very small portion of the law of instructions pitfalls seem inescapable. But when there is added the myriad of rules having to do with credibility of witnesses, presumptions, circumstantial evidence, degrees of proof, commenting on

---

69 MISS. CODE ANN. (1930) Sec. 586; see Watkins v. State, 60 Miss. 323 (1882).

70 Degonia v. St. Louis Rr. Co., 224 Mo. 564, 123 S. W. 807 (1909); Gracy v. Atlantic Rr. Co., 53 Fla. 350, 42 So. 903 (1907); Healea v. Keenan, Ex'r, 244 Ill. 484, 91 N. E. 646 (1910); Tullis v. Chase & Co., 162 Iowa, 264, 144 N. W. 17 (1913); Bowlin v. Archer, 157 Ky. 540, 163 S. W. 477 (1914); Riley v. City of Independence, 258 Mo. 671, 167 S. W. 1022 (1914); Swift v. Holoubek, 60 Neb. 784, 84 N. W. 249 (1900); Kirk v. Territory, 10 Okla. 46, 60 Pac. 797 (1900); Barker v. Coats, 34 S. D. 291, 148 N. W. 134 (1914); Smith v. Clark, 37 Utah 116, 106 Pac. 653 (1910).

71 See I BLASHFIELD, INSTRUCTIONS TO JURIES (1916) 177, n. 39 for a compilation of authorities.

72 Id. at 183, n. 67.

73 Id. at 233, n. 2.

74 Id. at 218, n. 1.

75 Id. at 335, n. 1.

76 Hayes v. Pennsylvania Rr. Co., 195 Pa. St. 184, 45 Atl. 925 (1900); Flowers v. Flowers, 92 Ga. 688, 18 S. E. 1006 (1893); Banner v. Schlessinger, 109 Mich. 262, 67 N. W. 116 (1896); Prine v. State, 73 Miss. 838, 19 So. 711 (1896).

the weight of the evidence or the sufficiency of it, cautionary instructions, etc.,—then one is tempted to picture the
trial judge's task as beset with the difficulties confronting
an amateur tight-rope walker.

The net result, however, is not to bring the trial judge
into disrepute, but rather to give unexpected functions to
instructions—to furnish trial judges with a means of con-
trolling the jury and to provide appellate courts with an
instrument whereby they control both the trial court and the
jury.

Although, under our system, it is deemed essential that
instructions be made intelligible to a jury,[77] there is no requirement that they be useful to a jury.[78] Whether or not
they can be useful to a jury will depend primarily upon
whether the crystallization of the law of the subject is such
that its rules may be reduced to intelligible propositions.
Take for comparison, the following two types of instructions as illustrative:

(1) "The court instructs the jury that if the plaintiffs were
taken over the farm by the defendants or (and) were shown the
bounds so that the plaintiffs knew where the farm was and what
was comprised within the bounds, it would not be of any consequence that representations may have been made by the defendants in relation to acreage."[79]

This instruction serves as a definite statement of the doctrine of *caveat emptor* in the law of vendor and purchaser.
When any given phase of the law is in such status that it is
capable of being reduced to such a criterion then it has at

---

[77] The function of instructions to serve as a guide to substantive principles of law, is well-recognized. This is attested by the general requirement
of separate findings of fact and specific declaration of law where the case is
tried without a jury. In at least one state (Maryland) it is required that
the court instruct itself as a jury. It is quite essential that the reviewing
court have access to the theories on which the case was tried. See Alexander
v. Capital Paint Co., 136 Md. 658, 111 Atl. 140 (1920); Richardson v. Anderson, 109 Md. 641, 72 Atl. 485 (1909); Murphy v. Smith, 112 Ill. App. 404
(1903); Harbison v. School District, 89 Mo. 184, 1 S. W. 30 (1886); White v.
Black, 115 Mo. App. 28, 90 S. W. 1153 (1905); McKeon v. McDermott, 22 Cal.
667 (1863); Shuler v. Lashhorn, 67 Kan. 694, 74 Pac. 264 (1903); Jennings v.
Frazier, 46 Ore. 470, 80 Pac. 1011 (1905); Kinn v. Nat'l Bank, 118 Wis. 537,
95 N. W. 969 (1903).

[78] "As I write these lines I hear that a very learned committee of the
American Bar is engaged on a re-statement of the law of torts. Nothing but
good can come from this if it is borne in mind that the object of any such statement is not to effect a verbal reconciliation of all the authorities but to frame
such a rule as a well-informed Court of last resort might lay down; and that,
if in any case the result is a proposition which cannot be made intelligible to
a jury, there is likely to be something wrong either with the drafting (which
should not happen to a committee including such expert draftsmen) or with
some of the less authoritative decisions." POLLOCK, LAW OF TORTS (13 ed.
1929) preface.

[79] Mabardy v. McHugh, 202 Mass. 148, 88 N. E. 894 (1909).

least some degree of predictability and applicable content.
But consider the next:

(2) ''Every person is negligent when, without intending to do
any wrong, he does such an act or omits to take such precaution
that under the circumstances he, as an ordinarily prudent person,
ought reasonably to foresee that he will thereby expose the interests of another to an unreasonable risk of harm. In determining whether his conduct will subject the interests of another to
an unreasonable risk of harm, a person is required to take into
account such of the surrounding circumstances as would be taken
into account by a reasonably prudent person and possess such
knowledge as is possessed by an ordinarily reasonable person and
to use such judgment and discretion as is exercised by persons
of reasonable intelligence under the same or similar circumstances.''[80]

This instruction was devised by Chief Justice Rosenberry
in a very scholarly attempt, based on the Restatement of
Negligence and other works, to re-define negligence in terms
of wrongful invasion of legally protected interests and the
consequences thereof. It was offered as preferable to an
instruction approved in a previous case,[81] which was criti-
cized because it indicated ''no standard by which the conduct of the defendant is to be measured''!

It is unnecessary to call attention to the fact that this
instruction makes the purported standard the ordinarily
prudent person, with the foresight, knowledge, judgment,
discretion and intelligence of a reasonable man. This means
that the jury, despite all efforts to the contrary, fixes the
standard of law which it will apply to the facts, or at least
that if the jurors pay any attention to the instruction at all,
they will use themselves as the standards by which to judge
the negligence of the defendant.[82] But appellate courts do
not really permit the jury to fix the standard, however
much they may appear to.[83] On appeal judges set themselves up as ordinarily prudent men and arrive at their
decision accordingly, though they may reason it in terms
of metaphysical distinctions. The standard loses all ob-
jectivity[84] as this ordinarily prudent person fades into
coincidence with the personality of the one judging, pro-
jected by imagination into the ''same or similar circum-

---

80 Osborne v. Montgomery, 203 Wis. 223, 234 N. W. 372 (1931).

81 Hamus v. Weber, 199 Wis. 320, 226 N. W. 392 (1929).

82 See Freeman v. Adams, 63 Cal. App. 225, 218 Pac. 600 (1923). But
see Grand Trunk Ry. Co. v. Ives, 144 U. S. 408 (1891); and see discussion in
GREEN, JUDGE AND JURY (1930) c. v, *The Negligence Issue.*

83 *Cf.* GREEN, *op. cit. supra* note 82, at 69, *The Duty Problem.*

84 See Seavey, *Negligence—Subjective or Objective* (1927) 41 HARV. L.
REV. 1.

stances", and becomes of little value as a principle guiding the jury.

Concerning the first illustrative instruction there may be differences of opinion as to what the law *ought* to be but there can be little room for doubt as to what the court has declared the law *is*. The factual issue is clear cut and its determination will automatically apply the law on account of the wording of the instruction. The respective functions of court and jury in actuality approach theoretical purpose. The verdict of the jury must necessarily reflect the finding of fact.

II

The Function of Instructions as A Method by Which Appellate Courts Control Juries and Trial Courts

Except for the hectic years immediately preceding and succeeding the Revolution of 1688, the English trial judges have exercised quite candidly a moderate and approved control over the jury. So it is with no surprise that we read in one of the early texts that:

"It is the practice for the judge at nisi prius not only to state to the jury all the evidence that has been given but to comment on its bearing and weight, and to state the legal rules upon the subject and their application to the particular case, and even to advise them as regards the verdict they should give, so that it may be in accord with his view of the law and justice; so that in effect, in general, the jury only give their opinion on the existence of the facts, and even then, in general, they follow the advice of the judge, and therefore in substance, the verdict is found or anticipated by the judge's direction, except indeed, as regards the amount of damages, and which also are greatly influenced by the observations of the judge, or may be corrected, if excessive or too small, by the Court in Banc."[85]

The pronounced fear and distrust of the power of judges evinced by the democratic temper, resulting in England in the mere passage of Fox's Libel Bill, found expression in America in innumerable statutes and constitutional provisions attempting to safeguard the power of juries in general. Moreover, England, despite its Revolution, never felt the sway of the spirit of the frontiersman to whom submission to any kind of court was to an extent a magnanimous compromise of individual sovereignty.

Shams permit the growth of social habits without revo-

---

85 3 CHITTY'S GENERAL PRACTICE (1836) 913. "Indeed without this assistance from the learned judge, few juries would, in a contested cause, be able to come to an unanimous opinion, being frequently left in a state of great perplexity by the influence of speeches of the contending leaders."

lutionary change. It is. trite to say that this is the secret of the adaptability of the common law procedure. American courts could not- forth-rightly overturn constitutional and statutory dogma that questions of fact are for the jury; and, as pointed out by Dean Green,[86] they least of all now are desirous of such drastic change. By upholding this sham, the appellate courts have been enabled actually to transform it into one of their most effective methods of control of both trial judges and juries.

It is possible that some of those who decry the use of juries and long for more power in the judges believe too literally the pronouncements of prohibitive strictures in decisions. It is an almost universal rule, imposed either by *stare decisis* or statute, that on appeal the court shall not weigh the evidence or, stated differently, that the findings of fact by a jury are binding and final. Yet this does not impede in any wise the examination of the instructions employed in the lower court. The court on appeal does not consider the verdict proper. Instead it philosophizes on whether or not the jury *might* have been misled by the error in the statement of the law, or whether or not they *might* have been influenced by an instruction which trenched in some manner on the province of fact, or whether or not they *might* have found differently had some requested instruction been given. The decision is that the learned trial judge erred in giving Instruction No. 12 or in refusing Instruction No. 18 and therefore the judgment should be reversed and a new trial granted.

On the other hand, if no fault can possibly be found with the ritual, which is well-nigh inconceivable, the appellate court which trusts in the constitution but keeps its powder dry, has no qualms of conscience about discovering that the jury manifestly failed to observe the directions of the trial judge—and this of course is strictly a matter of *law* and not of *fact*.

There are a number of other devices by which appellate courts have wrested control from trial judges and juries, but were they all abolished, it is probable that the errors of misdirection, non-direction and failure to observe directions would be sufficient to assure them such control. And this power, once garnered, is grudgingly surrendered even to legislative assault. Let the legislature attempt to restore some wonted prestige to the jury and such a decision as that in *Thoe v. C. M. St. Paul Railway Company*[87] will

---

86 GREEN, *op. cit. supra* note 82, at 375-376.
87 181 Wis. 456, 195 N. W. 407 (1923).

be forthcoming, wherein the court will rise to abide by its oath to uphold and maintain the constitution by preserving inviolate its power to reverse a judgment which is contrary to the evidence. Of course, should the organic law creating the court itself forbid the entertainment of a motion for a new trial based on the verdict being contrary to the evidence, the court may feel constrained to abide by the restriction, but nevertheless it may examine the evidence without compunction to determine whether on account of its lack, the verdict was contrary to law[88] or whether the jury failed to observe the directions of the court. These are questions of law and of the very essence of judicial power, which may even be implied from the constitutional division of government into three co-ordinate branches.

The federal courts, hampered only by the broad constitutional provision preserving the right of trial by jury, followed to an extent the English practice. They now consistently charge the jury orally, sum up the evidence, comment on it and even give the jury the benefit of opinion provided it is made clear that the jury is not to be controlled by it. And since the jurors are for the most part ordinary individuals, impressed by the solemnity and atmosphere of the court into an unwonted timidity and docility, the federal judge usually has it in his power, if he so wills, to mold a verdict in accord with his own views.

But to preserve trial by jury "inviolate" in the states, such practices as prevail in the federal courts were circumvented by various taboos. Quite the natural reaction of the state appellate courts then was to utilize these taboos and their power to protect the jury from inaccuracies of judicial statement to subjugate the trial court and jury.

Thus, the Supreme Court of California (Department One) held that the use of the disjunctive "or" between the words "aid" and "abet" was not fatal error, because to the ordinary mind one who aids or assists in the commission of forgery is guilty; and this is true because to such a mind criminality is included as an element in the act of the party aiding or assisting. But the court *en banc*, decided that the use of the disjunctive was prejudicial error because "the word 'aid' does not imply guilty knowledge or felonious intent, whereas the definition of the word 'abet' includes knowledge of the wrongful purpose of the perpetrator and counsel and encouragement in the crime."[89]

---

88 Monroe County v. Driskell, 3 Ga. App. 583 (1907).

89 People v. Dole, 122 Cal. 486, 55 Pac. 581 (1898); approved in 123 Cal. 403, 56 Pac. 44 (1899).

In a somewhat similar situation, the court of Montana expressed the attitude of the state courts generally in its gentle admonition: "In this connection we may observe that it is far safer for a trial court to make use of instructions generally approved by the courts rather than to risk the danger of invading the province of the jury by formulating new ones."[90] The use of instructions that have been repeated over and over is "the safe practice and obviates the necessity of a consideration of instructions on the subject differently worded."[91]

Thus are instructions reduced to formalism. From the taboos calculated to safeguard the province of the jury have been derived the means for surreptitiously scaling its walls. The original purpose of giving instructions for the actual enlightenment of the jury, to assist them in applying the law to the facts, has become inconsequential.[92]

The priests, however, are not fooled by the system evolved. The lawyers and judges are perfectly aware that juries pay scant attention to the type of instructions commonly given them on the law applicable to the facts, and that as a rule they are incapable of the fine discrimination such an application requires. But it is impressive to the public and it clothes the jurors with a sanctimonious mantle of enlightenment which gives them a sense of peace and accord with authority. Trial lawyers may consume a great deal of time on instructions, but little of it is wasted on attempting to force the jury's attention to them. It is usually as futile as reading a decision of the Supreme Court to a justice of the peace or arguing the Constitution with a policeman.

III

The Function of Instructions from the Lawyer's Viewpoint as Traps for the Courts

Under the common law the court has the right to instruct the jury of its own motion[93] and in some states it is under

---

90 State v. Allen, 34 Mont. 403, 87 Pac. 177 (1906). See also McQueary v. People, 48 Colo. 214, 110 Pac. 210 (1910); State v. Murray, 91 Mo. 95, 3 S. W. 397 (1886); Lawless v. State, 4 Lea 179 (Tenn. 1879).

91 Minich v. People, 8 Colo. 440, 9 Pac. 4 (1885). "Its very novelty was a sufficient reason for its refusal. It is a maxim of the law that 'the old way is the safe way.'" McAlpine v. State, 47 Ala. 78, 82 (1872). See also Berkovitz v. Gravel Co., 191 Cal. 195, 215 Pac. 675 (1923).

92 Anderson v. Horlick's Malted Milk Co., 137 Wis. 569, 579, 119 N. W. 342 (1909): "While a trial judge, as an original matter, may be able to state a rule of law more concisely and in language more easily understood by the ordinary juror than the examples given by this court for stating the same rule, such departures are to be avoided, generally speaking, since they are quite liable to result in just the difficulty we are now dealing with."

93 City of Chicago v. Keefe, 114 Ill. 222, 2 N. E. 267 (1885).

a duty to do so.[94]   But in all jurisdictions exceptions can be taken to instructions whether they be offered by court or by counsel, written or oral, in time or out.   They may also be suggested either in whole or in addition, so that ultimately the language, form and substance of the instruction or charge will be guided in large measure by the wit and ingenuity of counsel.   In those states where written instructions are required they are usually wholly devised and offered by counsel, subject to modification by the court.

Insofar as the lawyer is concerned, the least of his worries is the conveyance of a correct dissertation on the law to the jury *for* the jury.   For the instructions will profit him little if he has not been able to get in enough helpful evidence to enable him to appeal to the emotions of the jurors in his summation.   But what a grave error the grant or refusal of a phrase, or even a single word chosen from the host of others, can be made to appear to an appellate court in a brief!

For counsel having that side of the cause which is weaker in law or less captivating in emotion, instructions are an ever-present help in time of trouble.   He has everything to gain by requesting a great number.   Aside from the greater force on appeal thereby afforded his argument that the jury failed to observe the instructions granted, he has high hopes that a harassed trial judge will refuse at least a few, and the more the better.   Especially is this true in representing defendants in criminal and tort cases.   In criminal cases if the jury should acquit, any erroneous instructions will be no weapon for the state's attorney.   And in tort cases, a plaintiff who can not win in the first trial, while the story is fresh and the witnesses responsive, may be expected to fare no better after the facts are cold and some of the witnesses absent.   Moreover, most plaintiffs in tort cases, are not financially capable of sustained litigation and so the defendant's counsel is very careful to "perfect the record."   One of the prime attributes of such "perfection" is to have a grand climax of errors in granting or refusing instructions with the exceptions properly noted.[95]

---

94 People v. Byrnes, 30 Cal. 206 (1866); New London Water Comm'rs v. Robbins, 82 Conn. 623, 74 Atl. 938 (1910),; Central Rr. v. Harris, 76 Ga. 501 (1886); Tretter v. Chicago Ry. Co., 147 Iowa 375, 126 N. W. 339 (1910); Heilman v. Commonwealth, 84 Ky. 457, 1 S. W. 731 (1886); Maxwell v. Mass. Title Insurance Co., 206 Mass. 197, 92 N. E. 42 (1910).   In other states the rule is sometimes confined to criminal cases.   See BLASHFIELD, *op. cit. supra* note 71, at 358, notes 12 and 13.

95 "Counsel for the defendant will usually not be solicitous to have the court correct a mistake in his charge to the jury because in event of an un-

That "to launch such a mass of legal conundrums upon a court which can never enlighten a jury, but are drawn generally with the real, if not avowed purpose of getting error into the record and entangling the court in some technical contradiction that may be used in a higher court, is a perversion of the law of instructing juries", was discovered by the Illinois Appellate Court in 1885.[96] But the censure did not discourage subsequent counsel for defendants in that state,[97] and the appellate court, realizing the futility and impropriety of an arbitrary rule limiting the number, decided that "a trial judge in the throes accompanying the examination of fifty or more instructions has our sincere sympathy, but relief rests with counsel not with the court."[98]

The Missouri court in a similar situation lost patience with the trial court:

"The changes rung on all phases of this case, and some not of this case, remind one of what Judge Scott used to say was 'like the multiplication table set to music.' We have remonstrated with the trial courts for years about the great impropriety and frequent injustice resulting from writing or giving instructions by the acre, but without avail, and so resort must be had to more drastic measures. We therefore hold that the great number of instructions given in this instance, of itself, warrants a reversal of the judgment."[99]

If the jury is to be given a rounded view of the applicable law, it must get it from the trial judge, who is least prepared by immediate study and preparation for the task. The cause probably has original features but if the judge attempts original instructions, he will step into innumerable pitfalls of precedent. The plaintiff offers few suggestions, fearing these dangers. The defendant seductively offers many or perhaps indignantly demands them. Assuming that

---

favorable verdict, the erroneous instructions given to the jury may constitute reversible error and he will be able to overturn the verdict by a motion for a new trial or on appeal. In such case counsel cannot be expected to urge his objections very strenuously to an erroneous instruction. He will probably take an exception to the erroneous portion of the charge and let the matter rest there and if the plaintiff does not take steps to see that all erroneous instructions are corrected, the verdict of the jury will avail him nothing." CORNELIUS' TRIAL TACTICS (1932) 291.

96 Citizens Gaslight Association v. O'Brien, 19 Ill. App. 231 (1885).

97 Chicago Athletic Club v. Eddy Electric M'f'g Co., 77 Ill. App. 204 (1898) (84 instructions asked); La Salle Coal Co. v. Eastman, 99 Ill. App. 495 (1902) (93 instructions asked). See also Grudzinske v. Chicago Ry. Co., 165 Ill. App. 152 (1911); Casey v. Reedy Elevator Co., 166 Ill. App. 595 (1912).

98 Daily v. Smith-Hippen Co., 111 Ill. App. 319 (1903); see also Chicago City Ry. Co. v. Sandusky, 198 Ill. 400, 64 N. E. 990 (1902), aff'g 99 Ill. App. 164 (1900).

99 Sidway v. Missouri Land Co., 163 Mo. 342, 63 S. W. 705 (1901). For a full discussion see Note, Ann. Cas. 1918A, 1087.

they are all legally correct, there is still the hazard of error in influencing the jury, by repetition, to believe that the court is on the defendant's side. If the judge refuses some of them, he is no doubt walking into the trap as planned. If he modifies and combines several of them without technical error he is a genius. It is no wonder, then, that any action he may take will be couched as far as possible in ritualistic statement, with his whole attention fixed on the probable reaction of the appellate judges and not on the twelve good men and true.

And so the three officers of the court to whom is entrusted the duty of acquainting the jury with the law are too busily engaged in dealing with the importunate artifices which are employed for the benefit of the appellate court to attend the theoretical arts. It is not intended generally that the jury should get an enlightened dissertation on the law under our present system—and who wishes that they should?

IV

The Function of Instructions as A Method by Which the Trial Court Maintains Its Integrity

Although bearing the same label, there are two distinct types of instructions which are so different from all other members of the class, as to be commonly identified by the adjectives: *cautionary* and *peremptory*. The so-called cautionary instructions are not instructions of law, although occasionally they are mistaken and treated as such by appellate courts. They are in large part suggestive, psychological guides to bring into the open the possibility of unduly influential emotional ferment. They tend to put the jury in the right attitude insofar as their own consciences are concerned. But it is doubtful that the mere enunciation of rules can increase the measure of comprehension and inhibit the natural reactions to evidence, or regulate arbitrarily the interpretations which other minds will make on the expressions or directions theretofore voiced.

Chief Justice McBride of Oregon, after delivering an opinion on cautionary instructions, said:

"The writer when upon the circuit bench was in the habit of giving such an instruction as a matter of course in cases of this character and in trials of homicide, but it is not certain that it ever had a particle of effect, as no juryman is ever aware that his opinion is being affected by the subtle influence of sympathy."[100]

---

[100] Sheurmann v. Mathison, 67 Ore. 419, 136 Pac. 330 (1913).

It is difficult to conceive of the plegmatic utterance of such a bromide as, the jury "should not lose their heads and return a verdict for a lady on general principles,"[101] having any very serious chance of counteracting the tender sympathies of sturdy jurors.

But cautionary instructions are not confined to guarding against sympathy and prejudice. They fulfill a very distinct need for the trial court when it is called upon to rule on innumerable and unexpected questions of law from the beginning of the trial to the end. Especially is this true as to questions dealing with the taking of testimony, the predication of evidence, conformity to the pleadings and admission and competence generally. It is imperative that he make some immediate disposition of the problem if the trial is not to drag out interminably. In a vast number of instances, counsel have not foreseen the particular issue and their resulting argument substitutes vehemence for erudition. Many trial courts in such a dilemma adopt the crafty practice of admitting such questionable testimony for the time being, and then in the light of subsequent developments excluding such phases as seen incompetent by an instruction cautioning the jurors to disregard it[102] or limit their consideration of the testimony to particular purposes.[103] This may make the lawyer excepting tear his hair, since he realizes the great unlikelihood of the jury being able to divest itself of particular sentences heard in a composite narrative some time earlier. But it is a great thing for the trial court over whom hovers the omni-present, ominous cloud of reversal. With a fair amount of common sense and a modicum of "legal hunch", a trial judge can by means of cautionary instructions, knock innumerable props from under otherwise dynamic exceptions—leaving the record cured of a multitude of sins. Even an incursion into the province of the jury may be rectified by judiciously reminding the jurors that they are the sole judges of the facts[104] and they should not attempt to infer what the

---

101 But perhaps it did have some influence in the case in which it was uttered as the jury found against the lady. Bingham v. Bernard, 36 Minn. 114, 30 N. W. 404 (1886).

102 Foxworth v. Brown, 120 Ala. 59, 24 So. 1 (1897); Williams v. State, 107 Ga. 721, 33 S. E. 648 (1899); Chesapeake & Ohio Ry. Co. v. Stein, 142 Ky. 515, 134 S. W. 1169 (1911); State v McKowen, 126 La. 1075, 53 So. 353 (1910).

103 James v. State, 167 Ala. 14, 52 So. 840 (1910); People v. Gray, 66 Cal. 271, 5 Pac. 240 (1884); Porter v. State, 173 Ind. 694, 91 N. E. 340 (1910); State v. Collins, 121 N. C. 667, 28 S. E. 520 (1897); Farwell v. Warren, 51 Ill. 467 (1869); Giddings v. Baker, 80 Tex. 308, 16 S. W. 33 (1891); People v. Hagenow, 236 Ill. 514, 86 N. E. 370 (1908).

104 Doll v. Chicago Consolidated Traction Co., 153 Ill. App. 442 (1910).

court's opinion may be.[105] If counsel oversteps decorum in his speech to the jury, the trial judge may brush away his sophistries,[106] weaken his protestations,[107] or possibly cure his improprieties by a word of warning to the jury.[108]

Cautionary instructions, of which there are many others not indicated in the foregoing, are generally held to be within the discretion of the trial court.[109] This adds excellence to their use as weapons to fend off the technical designs of the lawyer on appeal, however trivial their effect may be in influencing the jury.

Mention has already been made of that other very significant weapon which the trial court has developed for the maintenance of its integrity by overt direction of the verdict —the peremptory instruction. The use of this device seems to have developed alongside the obsolescence of the demurrer to evidence and some courts apply the same test.[110] Various other tests are applied, such as scintilla of evidence [111] and reasonable inference,[112] but the results are very much the same and the general rule is that a verdict should be directed if a contrary finding of the jury would be set aside.[113] It is also generally held that the court has no right to direct a verdict of guilty in a criminal trial,[114]

---

105 North Chicago Street Rr. Co. v. Kaspers, 186 Ill. 246, 57 N. E. 849 (1900).

106 State v. Way, 38 S. C. 333, 347, 17 S. E. 39 (1892).

107 Smith v. State, 95 Ga. 472, 20 S. E. 275, 20 S. E. 291 (1894).

108 Morehouse v. Remson, 59 Conn. 392, 22 Atl. 427 (1890).

109 Day v. State, 54 Fla. 25, 44 So. 715 (1907); State v. Barton, 70 Ore. 470, 142 Pac. 348 (1914). City of Tacoma v. Wetherby, 57 Wash. 295, 106 Pac. 903 (1910); Birmingham Fire Insurance Co. v. Pulver, 126 Ill. 329, 18 N. E. 804 (1888); Dinsmore v. State, 61 Neb. 418, 85 N. W. 445 (1901).

110 Anderson v. Southern Cotton Oil Co., 73 Fla. 432, 74 So. 975 (1917); Chicago Bank v. Northwestern National Bank, 152 Ill. 296, 38 N. E. 739 (1894); Hayward v. North Jersey Street Ry. Co., 74 N. J. L. 678, 65 Atl. 737 (1906).

111 People v. People's Insurance Exchange, 126 Ill. 466, 18 N. E. 774 (1888); Anfensen v. Banks, 180 Iowa 1066, 163 N. W. 608 (1917).

112 Philadelphia Rr. Co. v. Gatta, 4 Boyce 38 (Del. 1913), 85 Atl. 721; Habeck v. Chicago Ry. Co., 146 Wis. 645, 132 N. W. 618 (1911).

113 Empire State Cattle Co. v. Atchison Ry. Co., 210 U. S. 1 (1907); Bell v. Carter, 164 Fed. 417 (C. C. A. 8th, 1908); Livesay v. Denver Bank, 36 Colo. 526 (1906); Wolf v. Chicago Co., 233 Ill. 501, 84 N. E. 614 (1908); Moore v. McKenney, 83 Me. 80. 21 Atl. 749 (1890); Lutz v. Atlantic Rr. Co., 6 N. M. 496, 30 Pac. 912 (1892); Supreme Tribe v. Owens, 50 Okla. 629, 151 Pac. 198 (1915); Dwight v. Germania Life Insurance Co., 103 N. Y. 341, 8 N. E. 654 (1886); Hemmens v. Nelson, 138 N. Y. 517, 34 N. E. 642 (1893); Morris v. Warwick, 42 Wash. 480, 85 Pac. 48 (1906); Norvell v. Kanawha Rr. Co., 67 W. Va. 467, 68 S. E. 288 (1910).

114 Sparf v. U. S., supra note 50; Konda v. U. S., 166 Fed. 91 (C. C. A. 7th, 1908); State v. Koch, 33 Mont. 490, 85 Pac. 272 (1905) State v. Godwin, 145 N. C. 461, 59 S. E. 132 (1907). The Arkansas court has held that even a verdict of guilty may be directed, where the punishment does not include imprisonment. Paxton v. State, 114 Ark. 393, 170 S. W. 80 (1914).

although the direction in favor of the accused is both frequent and unquestioned.[115]

The peremptory instruction has become so unrelated to all other types of instructions that it is now seldom treated under that classification. Of course it is a palpable invasion of the "province" of the jury and in direct contravention to those rules which are ordinarily regarded as fundamental.[116] Its progress from the scintilla rule through the equivalent of the demurrer to evidence concept, to setting aside the verdict, has got it where the most elegant circumlocution would be required to make it appear other than an infringement.[117] While the warrant for a directed verdict on the ground that if a contrary verdict were returned the court would be under necessity of setting it aside, seems logical enough in the setting of present-day attitudes, there is a vast difference. Setting aside the verdict means a new trial by a new jury with time intervening for mutations in evidential strengths with always the possibility of compromise; but a directed verdict constitutes res adjudicata.[118]

---

[115] Jackson v. State, 178 Ala. 76, 60 So. 97 (1912); State v. McCaffrey, 181 Ind. 200, 103 N. E. 801 (1914); People v. Minney, 155 Mich. 534, 119 N. W. 918 (1909); Isbell v. U. S., 227 Fed. 788 (C. C. A. 8th, 1915); State v. Torello, 100 Conn. 637, 124 Atl. 375 (1924); State v. Gomez, 58 Mont. 177, 190 Pac. 982 (1920); Stare v. McHenry, 93 W. Va. 396, 117 S. E. 143 (1923); State v. Myer, 69 Iowa 148, 28 N. W. 484 (1886); Combs v. Commonwealth, 162 Ky. 86, 172 S. W. 101 (1915); State v. Grondin, 113 Me. 479, 94 Atl. 947 (1915); State v. Young, 237 Mo. 170, 140 S. W. 873 (1911); People v. Ledwon, 153 N. Y. 10, 46 N. E. 1046 (1897); State v. Norman, 153 N. C. 591, 68 S. E. 917 (1910); State v. Fiester, 32 Ore. 254, 50 Pac. 551 (1897); Devoy v. State, 122 Wis. 148, 99 N. W. 455 (1904).

[116] In the earlier cases even where a verdict was directed in civil matters it was considered that the direction must be that if the jury believed all the testimony they should so find, otherwise the court would be infringing on the inherent right of the jury to pass on the credibility of the witnesses. See again the opinion in 11 Fed. 478 (C. C. R. I. 1882). See also Gwyn Harper Co. v. Carolina Central Rr., 128 N. C. 280, 38 S. E. 894 (1901). Under present practice the instruction is a mere matter of form after the motion is granted and judgment is usually given regardless of what the jury may think. When a peremptory instruction is granted, the jury may even be compelled to return a verdict accordingly. Curran v. Stein, 110 Ky. 99, 60 S. W. 839 (1901); W. B. Grimes Dry Goods Co. v. Malcolm, 164 U. S. 483 (1896). Or the court may direct entry of verdict without their assent. Cahill v. Chicago etc. Ry. Co., 74 Fed. 285 (C. C. A. 7th, 1896). See also In re Sharon's Estate, 179 Cal. 447, 177 Pac. 283 (1918); Banfill v. Byrd, 122 Miss. 288, 84 So. 227 (1920); Kirshenbaum v. Mass. Bonding etc. Co., 107 Neb. 494, 186 N. W. 529 (1922).

[117] But cf. Catlett v. St. Louis Ry. Co., 57 Ark. 461, 21 S. W. 1062 (1893); Hopkins v. Nashville Rr. Co., 96 Tenn. 409, 34 S. W. 1029 (1896).

[118] Denver v. Home Savings Bank, 200 Fed. 28, (C. C. A. 8th, 1912) aff'd, 236 U. S. 101 (1915); In re Sharon's Estate, supra note 116; Andrews v. School District, 35 Minn. 70, 27 N. W. 303 (1886); Dunseth v. Butte Electric Ry. Co., 41 Mont. 14, 108 Pac. 567 (1910); Reams v. Sinclair, 97 Neb. 542, 150 N. W. 826 (1915); Wicks v. Sanborn, 72 Ore. 321, 143 Pac. 1007 (1914); H. F. Watson Co. v. Citizens Concrete Co., 28 R. I. 472, 68 Atl. 310 (1907);

To the ordinary mind, all the reasons for directing a verdict for the plaintiff in a civil suit apply with equal cogency to the direction of a verdict for the state. In a criminal trial and in one of the earlier cases on the subject, Circuit Justice Hunt so far lost his judicial equilibrium over the unheard of temerity of a female by the name of Susan B. Anthony, who, knowing she was a woman, yet had the effrontery to vote in a congressional election, that he came right out and reasoned along such lines to sustain his action in having directed the jury to find her guilty.[119] This grave error in presuming that there was no distinction between the inviolability of jury trials in civil cases and in criminal cases, was of course unpardonable, particularly at a time when the judiciary was quietly curbing the jury in civil cases without disturbing the public mind. The worst of it was that his deductions appeared unanswerable in view of the precedents as to the duty of the jury to take the law from the court.[120] But a few years later matters were very neatly set back into their former paths by Justice McCrary in a decision which became the leading case on the rule that verdicts can not be directed for the state in a criminal case. This decision deserves a large place in our legal history as a monumental example of judicial ingenuity in reconciling conflicting principles for the purpose of preserving expeditious tendencies. After a facile discourse on constitutional provisions and the respective provinces of the court and jury the justice offers this unexpected yet judicially satisfactory solution:

"It is now well settled in civil cases, where the facts are undisputed and the case turns upon questions of law, the court may direct a verdict in accordance with its opinion of the law; but the authorities which settle this rule have no application to criminal cases. In a civil case the court may set aside the verdict, whether it be for the plaintiff or defendant, upon the ground that it is contrary to the law as given by the court; but in a criminal case if the verdict is one of acquittal, the court has no power to set it aside. It would be a useless form for a court to submit a civil case involving only questions of law to the consideration of a jury, where the verdict when found, if not in accordance with the court's view of the law would be set aside. The same result is accomplished by an instruction given in advance to find a verdict in accordance with the court's opinion of the law. But not so in

McCown v. Muldrow, 91 S. C. 523, 74 S. E. 386 (1912), Morgan v. Chicago Ry. Co., 83 Wis. 348, 53 N. W. 741 (1892).

119 24 Fed. Cas. 829 (1873).

120 On reflection, however, Justice Hunt seems to have relented for in the trial of the election officers growing out of the same matter, he modified his instruction. 11 Fed. 470, 473 (C. C. Kan. 1882).

criminal cases. **A verdict of acquittal cannot be set aside and therefore if the court can direct a verdict of guilty, it can do indirectly that which it has no power to do directly.**"[121]

On such a foundation much of the later law of peremptory instructions or directed verdicts has been built. Since there can be no directed verdicts for the state in criminal cases the integrity of jury trials has been preserved as a sop to traditional guaranties; but the inroads upon jury trials in civil cases have been considerable by both courts and legislatures. It is probable that, in an age when juries are coming more and more into disrepute as a drag on efficient administration, the possibilities of peremptory instructions will be more deeply probed. An observation of the cases in the last decade will convince one that direction of the verdict is fast becoming one of the most customary and efficient tools of the trial court.

V

Procedural Problems Arising as A Result and the Escapes from these Problems.

A critical examination of a decision seldom reveals the precarious snares baited for appellate judges. Neither does it reveal their extremity at times in extricating themselves in accordance with their convictions and yet in a rational manner. Many appellate judges no doubt suffer from conflicts between the past promises of *stare decisis* and the present virtues of personal conviction. Some blindly follow a literal interpretation of precedent and justify themselves with loyalty to their oaths. Others follow conscience and rationalize as best they can, or overrule as occasion requires. Still others, with more of a penchant for "state-craft," shape the materiality of the facts to fit the salient principles of the past and in this manner forecast what they consider the genius of the law— at the same time preserving their sacred oaths unsullied. But regardless of methods, on them is cast the ultimate responsibility of weaving the seamless web. An enumerated treatment of the obvious specific problems suggested by the varied functions of instructions would result in too burdensome a reiteration of much of the matter hereinbefore detailed. A few general observations should suffice to terminate this discussion.

The fallacy of the use of law and fact as a categorical test for the various phases of jury trial was effectively shown by Dean Thayer in an excellent article published in

---

121 *Id.* at 474 (Italics supplied).

1890, in which he pointed out that a great deal of confusion resulted from defining the terms in verbal equivalents.[122] More recently Dean Green has discussed the desirability of such expansible and collapsible terms which elude the strictures of definitive bonds:

"No two terms of legal science have rendered better service than 'law' and 'fact'. They are basic assumptions; irreducible minimums and the most comprehensive maximums at the same instant. They readily accommodate themselves to any meaning we may desire to give them. In them and their kind a science of law finds its strength and durability. They are the creations of centuries. What judge has not found refuge in them? The man who could succeed in defining them would be a public enemy. They may torture the souls of language mechanicians who insist that all words and phrases must have a fixed content but they and their flexibility are essential to the science which has to do with the control of men through power to pass judgment on their conduct."[123]

Dean Green further develops these terms in the allocation of the functions of judge and jury generally and with particularity in deceit, assault and battery, and malicious prosecution.[124]

Professor Bohlen considers the dissertation on law and fact the least satisfactory of Dean Green's book.[125] But be that as it may, the criticism merely emphasizes the more important point that there continue to be many cavil-breeding procedural problems which result from the piling up of decisions based on the province of court and jury. Law and fact are used as the basic criterions for the content of instructions and charges which in turn become devices for the variety of untheoretical uses and functions in the hands of trial judges, lawyers and appellate courts. And aside from the procedural confusion, there is the assertedly graver problem of the crystallization of rules, preventing growth to meet new social developments.

Professor Bohlen, as he himself indicates in his review of Dean Green's book,[126] has considered these matters with respect to negligence (though not specifically from the standpoint of instructions) in his "Mixed Questions of Law

---

122 "But if we ask the question what sort of thing it is that is for the court and what for the jury, we do not get on, for we are told that matters of law are for the court and matters of fact for the jury, ad questionem, etc. . . . We do not then escape the necessity of trying to determine what is a matter of fact and what is a matter of law." Thayer, *Law and Fact in Jury Trials* (1890) 4 HARV. L. REV. 147.

123 Green, *op. cit supra* note 82, at 270.

124 *Id.* at 278 *et seq.*

125 (1932) 80 U. OF PA. L REV. 783.

126 *Ibid.*

and Fact.''[127]   In the tendency of the courts to usurp the
functions of the jury in the fixing of negligence standards
he sees two great dangers:
(1) ''undue rigidity which results from the unfortunate feeling
that any decision of a court creates a rule of law which, as law,
is absolutely and eternally valid''; and (2) the fixing of ''standards of conduct so definite and precise as to give to unscrupulous
practitioners extraordinary opportunities for the successful
coaching of witnesses.''
Finally, he hopes that in the usurpation of this function of
the jury, the courts will realize that ''they are exercising
an administrative function and that such decisions are not
like their decisions declaring those principles which are
fundamental to our concept of law, sacrosanct from judicial
re-examination and change under changing conditions.''

The second danger suggested by Professor Bohlen may
be dismissed with few words. It is patent that there is
presently less precision in the law of negligence as to
standards of conduct than in any other branch of the law.
Yet no unscrupulous lawyer being a ''reasonable man''
should anticipate any greater difficulty in coaching a witness in such manner as easily to ''escape a non-suit or a
directed verdict for the defendant.'' The net difference,
if any, is probably to cause the manufacture of a much
better quality of lie for the sake of safety. But admitting
the efficacy of this danger, the courts cannot very well
afford to adopt the policy of either retaining a standard
in its own bosom for fear the unscrupulous lawyer will
learn what it is, or occasionally overruling a prior decision
in order to bring him up with a jerk.

As to the first danger and the suggestion advanced,
Professor Bohlen perhaps overlooks the manner in which
lawyers and judges work and have worked since time im-
memorial. There is apparently nothing more hateful and
ill-advised to them than a frontal attack on a problem. It
simply does not jibe with the legal mind or the spirit of our
system. Flanking movements have made the significant
history of our law, to the amazement and occasional disgust
of all except those who practice it. In stating the danger,
Professor Bohlen himself suggests the antipathy for change
but he fails to take into account that even if a rule which has
become a ''scandal and a hissing'' goes for a long time un-
changed, it does not follow that its force persists un-
impaired when once the court has become convinced of its
pernicious social value. Has any ingenious judge had

127 (1924) 72 U. OF PA. L. REV. 111.

serious difficulty in accomplishing desired results in-directly?

The courts have sufficient means of administration. What they need is convictive guidance; direction is more important than directness. Appellate judges could scarcely wish for freer rein in causes tried by juries. While the myriad of precise rules laid down for the instruction of juries and the apparent impossibility of satisfying all of them in a particular case would seem to have reduced the procedure to such precarious technicalities that the ap-pellate court would be bound to grant a new trial, yet every-one knows such is not the truth. Misdirection, non-direc-tion and failure to observe directions were manufactured by the courts themselves from the raw materials of law and fact for the control of others, and it should not be expected that clever courts will be entrapped in their own devices. There are three more or less arbitrary escapes by which the judgment of the lower court may be affirmed without even leaving the semblance of a track: (1) by ignoring questions raised in the record, (2) memorandum decisions and (3) discretionary appeals. None of these, however, is the prevailing mode. The use of the two latter will no doubt receive favorable expansion as the appalling rate of printed reports renders some such drastic action necessary. But by far the most frequently used now is that ubiquitous exit, non-prejudicial error,[128] at the door of which the unanswerable logic of an appeal brief premised on *stare decisis* falls.

---

128 It should be noted that the verdict is now tested by the courts con-, sidering whether or not the jury *was* misled instead of whether it *may* have been misled. A host of authorities may be found for harmless and non-prejudicial error under *Appeal and Error* in the AMERICAN DIGEST SYSTEM and CORPUS JURIS as well as in other standard works. Of course some states have provision for it by constitution and statute, (*e.g.*, CAL. CONST. art. VI. Sec. 4½), but since the provision is made flexible enough so that injustice may not result, the decisions are scarcely different from those of other states having no such written provision. This may be seen from a casual perusal of TREAD-WELL'S ANNOTATIONS (6th ed. 1931).

MODERN TENDENCIES IN PREPARATION FOR THE BAR

By WILL SHAFROTH*

When Professor Langdell inaugurated the case system of study in 1871 at the Harvard Law School, he revolutionized methods of law teaching. His statement in the preface to his first case book on contracts that

"Law considered as a science consists of certain principles or doctrines. To have such mastery of these as to be able to apply them with constant facility and certainty to the ever-tangled skein of human affairs is what constitutes· a true lawyer; and hence to acquire that mastery should be the business of every earnest student of law"

still remains as a lode-stone to guide the intending candidate for a lawyer's license. This means, if it means anything, that a student is not to be crammed with raw information, but that he is to be given a course which will develop in him effective knowledge.

But while this truth still marches on, methods of effectuating the desired result are changing. The case system is being subjected to some criticism as not being ideal for use during the entire three years of law study. Furthermore, the functional aspects of the law are being emphasized, and its relation to the social sciences is receiving much more consideration by the law schools than it ever has before. More specialized courses and research work of various kinds are being made part of the curriculum in some law schools. At the University of Minnesota and at Northwestern University four year courses are now given in the law school. Legal aid clinics which have proven their usefulness and practicability, where the students actually handle the work themselves, have been established at the law schools of Northwestern University, University of Cincinnati, University of Southern California, and Harvard, and are being tried out in more than half a dozen other schools. Organizations such as the student Bar Association at Duke University have been formed to develop professional spirit among the law students, and the Society of Law Alumni of the University of Pennsylvania has proved itself invaluable to the profession by under-

*Adviser to the Council of the American Bar Association on Legal Education and Admissions to the Bar.

taking the task of providing sponsors for law students in that state.

But change has not been confined to methods of teaching and alteration of curriculum in law schools. Many of the old ideas in reference to the most efficient kind of training for practice at the bar have radically changed since the beginning of this century. If we go back to 1890 we find there were only 4,400 students in law schools. Undoubtedly the number who were studying law in offices at that time was considerably greater. Today the number of law school students is about ten times that many, while the number of law office students has dwindled to an almost negligible three or four per cent. The reason for this is obvious. While formerly a student in a law office got actual instruction and help from the practitioner with whom he worked and learned while he wrote out contracts and deeds at his senior's direction, today he is a mere cog in the wheel and if he has not some knowledge of law he becomes more of a hindrance than a help. The apprentice system is gone, and with it we have lost some of the great benefits to be derived from the association by a young man with a practitioner of standing. But in its place we have institutions equipped with experts in teaching, specialists in the particular phases of law in which they instruct, and we have students who come with a background of general education, prepared to give such time as is necessary to master the profession they intend to enter.

Although there have been many changes over the last few decades, as early as 1881 a resolution was passed by the American Bar Association on the recommendation of its Committee on Legal Education and Admissions to the Bar, recommending a three years' course in law schools.[1] In 1897 the additional prerequisite of a high school education before law training was added.[2] It was only in the last decade, however, that any very considerable attention was given to the requirements for admission to the bar. In 1921 a committee under the chairmanship of Hon. Elihu Root recommended and secured the adoption by the American Bar Association of standards of legal education providing for two years of pre-legal college education or its equivalent before the study of law, and graduation from an approved school having a three year law course if the students gave all of their time to its study, or a four year course if the school was on a part time basis. At the time

---

1 Vol. IV, Reports of the American Bar Association (1881), p. 28.
2 Vol. XX, Reports of the American Bar Association (1897), pp. 31, 33.

this resolution was adopted no state required more than a high school education for admission to the bar, but today there are nineteen states where either presently or prospectively the requirement is that the applicant for the bar must have at least two years of college work or its equivalent in addition to law training.[3]

Opponents of this program of the American Bar Association struggled against it unceasingly but without avail, and at the annual meeting of that body at Memphis in 1929 it was reaffirmed with overwhelming emphasis. Progress in the adoption of these standards, while not spectacular, has been steady, and in many states where these recommendations of general education or legal training have not been passed by the legislature or incorporated into the rules of the courts of last resort the state bar associations have gone on record as favoring them.[4]

Various arguments have been advanced pointing to the desirability of not making it too difficult to acquire a license to practice law. It is said that the door of opportunity must be left open and the poor boy as well as the rich boy must be given a chance to enter the legal profession. The examples of Abraham Lincoln, of John Marshall and of Grover Cleveland have often been given, and when Silas Strawn was president of the Bar Association and carrying on a very aggressive campaign to advance the qualifications for admission, he was pointed to as a shining example of what could be accomplished by a man without a college education. I do not think it is necessary to dwell on these arguments at any great length, as they have been repeatedly discussed before. At the time of Lincoln, and Marshall, and even in Grover Cleveland's time, a college education was a very difficult thing to acquire. It was then, in truth, the luxury of the rich. But even since 1890, the enrollment in our colleges and universities has increased over fivefold, while the population has only doubled, and today it is estimated by one of the high officials of the Bureau of Education of the government that in the colleges and universities of this country as a whole one-fifth of the men and one-tenth of the women are entirely self-support-

---

3 Colorado, Connecticut, Delaware, Idaho, Illinois, Kansas, Michigan, Minnesota, Montana, New Jersey, New York, North Dakota, Ohio, Pennsylvania, Rhode Island, Washington, West Virginia, Wisconsin, and Wyoming.
4 Arizona, California, Florida, Georgia, Iowa, Louisiana, Missouri, Nebraska, Nevada, North Carolina, South Carolina, South Dakota, Utah, and Virginia.

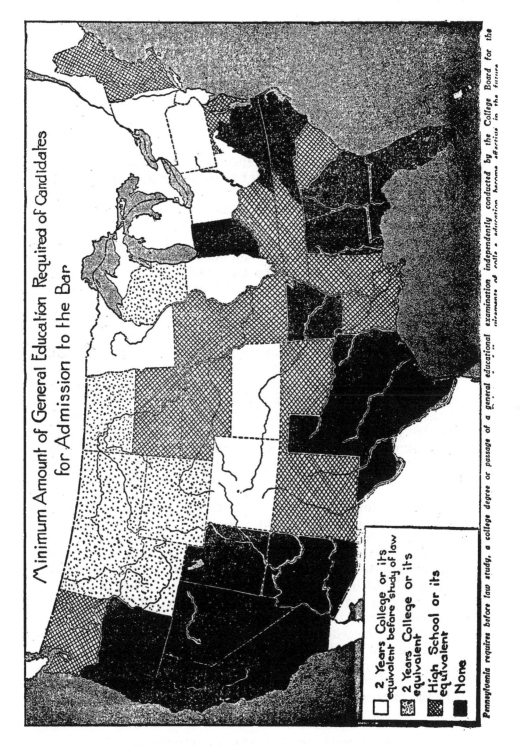

Minimum Amount of General Education Required of Candidates for Admission to the Bar

☐ 2 Years College or its equivalent before study of law

▨ 2 Years College or its equivalent

▧ High School or its equivalent

■ None

Pennsylvania requires before law study, a college degree or passage of a general educational examination independently conducted by the College Board for the requirements of college education become effective in the future

ing, while one-half of the men and one-fourth of the women are contributing to their support by working part of the time.[5] There seems to be no question that a man of ambition today can secure a college education whether his family can afford to pay his way through college or not. The opportunities are so vastly greater in this direction than they were forty or fifty years ago that a comparison is entirely beside the point.

But the argument misses the mark for another reason also. It is true even today that there are many exceptional men who could study law in their own homes without ever having attended college at all and pass a creditable bar examination and become leading members of the bar. These are the men with the ambition, the purpose and the drive to succeed. But they are not the ones whom the profession is seeking to keep out of the bar, and it is also true that they will not be kept out by restrictions requiring a college education or a definite direction as to how law study shall be pursued. They are the kind of men who surmount obstacles and who achieve their ultimate aim. But the object of the standards above referred to is to bar out men of inferior mental capacity and those whose ethical standards may be open to question. They are what might be called the lower fringe; they are willing to become lawyers if they can do it without great sacrifice. They can perhaps acquire enough legal knowledge by their own study and by cramming to pass the bar examinations, but some of them at least will never be properly qualified lawyers. It is against them the public must be protected.

Are we going to say that because we have the example of one or a dozen brilliant men who have reached the heights of the profession although they knew very little law when they were admitted to practice, that, therefore, this should be the rule for everyone? Remember that our object should be to make every licensed attorney a person fit to advise a client on the law in important matters and capable of resisting temptations that may be put in the way of anyone who handles important matters. Rules for admission to the bar cannot be based on the accomplishments of the most highly gifted in a class; rather they must be designed to keep out the lowest group in a class, as they are the ones who will damage the public and the profession.

---

5 Greenleaf, Walter J., *Self-Help for College Students*, pp. 58-64.

Bar examinations by themselves are far from an infallible test of legal knowledge. In New York, for example, it is said that the students who take a certain cram course increase their chances of passing the bar examinations by ten per cent. Is it possible to argue that this six weeks of preparation really adds ten per cent to their knowledge of the law? But nevertheless bar examinations if combined with adequate qualifications of preliminary education and legal training form the best measure which we are able to make of young men who want to be lawyers. With the bar becoming daily more overcrowded the necessity for such qualifications is becoming continually more apparent.

In the last issue of "Notes on Legal Education," published by the Council of the American Bar Association on Legal Education and Admissions to the Bar, this subject is dealt with in the following language:

"Chief Judge Benjamin N. Cardozo of the New York Court of Appeals, whose recent appointment to the Supreme Court of the United States won the enthusiastic approbation of the legal profession, in an address delivered at the dedication of the new building of the New York County Lawyer's Association on May 26, 1930,* brought out the contrast between the overcrowded condition of the bar of today and the situation two hundred years ago, in the following words: 'In 1695 there were only forty-one lawyers in New York, and litigants with money used to retain the whole bar of the locality, leaving no one for their adversaries. Accordingly in the same year an act was adopted by the assembly of the Province to regulate the number of lawyers that any litigant might retain, just as laws were enacted to regulate the enjoyment of other luxuries of life. The number was fixed at two. 'If they retain any more,' said the statute, 'it shall be lawful for the justices of the Bench where the suit is depending to order all such attorneys as shall be retained, more than two as aforesaid, to plead for the other side, without returning the fee received, anything contained in this or any other act to the contrary hereof in any wise notwithstanding.' There was poetic justice for you! Lawyer number 3 or lawyer number 4, retained and paid by an enthusiastic plaintiff, might turn up on the day of the trial, the money in his pocket, espousing the cause of the defendant. What would our

---

* Contained in the collection of essays and addresses of Judge Cardozo published under the title "Law and Literature."

Grievance Committee have to say about such practices today? I must admit that in my judgment it would have
been fairer, if every client was limited to two lawyers, to
provide that every lawyer should be furnished with two
clients. Very likely such a guaranty is a blessing too great
to be attainable in any earthly commonwealth. At any rate
the lawyers seem to have worried along without it. I wish
the draftsmen of the act of 1695 could have a look at us
today.'

"If they could look at us today, they would see a national
bar of approximately one hundred and sixty thousand lawyers—with forty thousand more students in law schools
on their way to join the ranks—almost universally ac-
knowledging that their profession is overcrowded, and yet
continuing to admit between nine and ten thousand new
licensees every year. They would see bar associations passing resolutions favoring higher standards (14 state bar
associations in states not having the two years college requirement have approved the American Bar Association
standards) yet courts hesitant about adopting them for
fear of offending the great god Demos, and legislatures
still contending for the 'open door' to the bar. They would
see bar examiners, who as a class are closer to the problem
than anyone else, and thus have a better realization of the
true situation, raising their barrier year by year and turning back over half of the candidates at every examination
in a vain effort to erect a dam against the flood of un-
qualified applicants.

"There are four agencies which can exercise some measure of control over this situation: the law schools, the courts,
the legislatures and the bar examiners. The law schools
are the agency through which ninety-five per cent of the candidates for the bar pass. If their standards were so strict
as to exclude all the unfit—and this should be done as early
as possible in the law school course—they could solve the
problem. But there is no organization including all the
schools through which they can act as a unit. Any tighten-
ing of standards on the part of the best schools inevitably
drives many of the poorer students into the poorer schools,
but does not improve the quality of the total body of
candidates or reduce their numbers.

"Many schools which have a preponderance of part time
teachers on their faculties lag behind in their entrance
requirements, in their equipment and in the quality of work
demanded from their students, although in a great many

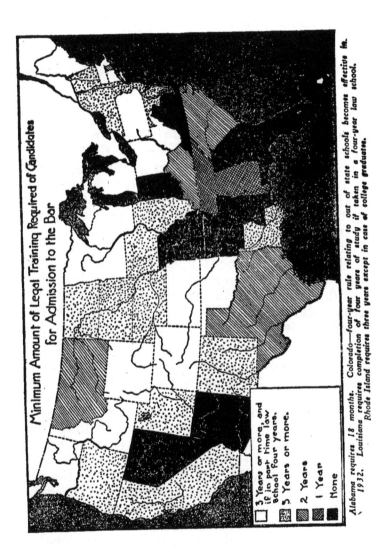

Minimum Amount of Legal Training Required of Candidates for Admission to the Bar

3 Years or more, and if in part-time law school four years.
5 Years or more.
2 Years
1 Year
None

Alabama requires 18 months. Colorado—four-year rule relating to out of state schools becomes effective in 1932. Louisiana requires completion of four years of study if taken in a four-year law school. Rhode Island requires three years except in case of college graduates.

cases these part time teachers are among the most influential practicing lawyers and judges in the community.
The fact is that they often teach because they regard it as
a duty they owe to the profession, and because of the real
inspiration and enjoyment they get from contact with
young men. But while in one way they are doing a duty
to the bar, in another they are neglecting their duty when
they do not insist that the school in which they teach maintain proper standards for admission of students, and re-
spectable standards of scholarship after they have been
admitted.

"The second agency is the courts, and the record shows
that where they have laid down rules of admission, standards of general education and legal training are higher than
where the legislature has undertaken to fix them. The
courts are generally conservative but mainly they are held
back by the fear that if they try to advance too rapidly,
the legislature will undo not only their latest step, but also
much of the progress which has been previously made.
These fears are perhaps in some cases well founded, but
where higher standards have the whole hearted backing of
the bar, the court can count upon their support and is
fully justified in placing upon the lawyers themselves the
burden of defending any increase of qualifications which
the court lays down. In other words, the court with the bar
behind it should lead the public rather than wait to follow
it.

"The third agency, the legislature, generally has the
Jacksonian idea that the practice of law should be open to
everyone who aspires to it. It looks on an increase of
lawyers as merely tending to augment the supply, thus
bringing about the wholly desirable result of lowering the
cost of legal services. It ignores the fact that incompetents
do the public much more harm than the benefits it could
hope to derive through decreased costs, both by the giving
of bungling advice and inadequate service, and through the
lowering of the moral standards of the marginal lawyer
which is the regrettable yet almost inevitable accompani-
ment of greatly increased competition in the legal profession.

"The fourth agency referred to is the Board of Bar
Examiners. Timid courts have said to their Boards, 'You
take the burden. Raise the standards of your examinations
and restrict the numbers admitted. We will support you
in it.' The bar examiners have responded nobly, not be-

cause they believed that their examinations could alone be
an infallible test of fitness to practice law, but because they
saw with their own eyes that many men were being admitted
to practice who could never be competent lawyers.   Even
this barrier the persistent candidate can often overcome,
particularly in jurisdictions where there is no rule pro-
hibiting an indefinite number of re-examinations for the
man who fails.

"Strict examinations alone will not accomplish the desired ends.   Nor will high qualifications for admission do
so by themselves.   The American Bar Association saw this
when it adopted the standards which Elihu Root's committee set up in 1921—first, two years of college education or
its equivalent; second, completion of a three year course
in an approved full time law school or a four year course
in an approved part time school; and third, passage of the
bar examinations.

"A great deal of progress has been made during the last
ten years, but much still remains to be done, and it is only
by working through the law schools, courts, legislatures and
examiners, that the desired ends can be obtained.   Three
of these four agencies are competent parts of the legal
profession, and the fourth is made up largely from its members.   Until the bar makes use of them to improve present
conditions, it will deserve at least some of the things which
are being said about it.   Senator George Wharton Pepper,
in a brilliant address before the recent annual dinner of
the New York State Bar Association, referred to this in
the following language:

" 'If we lawyers judge ourselves we are apt to betray
a foible for self-appreciation.   Perhaps this is a mistake
that our banking friends made until they were startled by
seeing themselves mirrored in the glassy surface of their
frozen assets.   It is better, therefore, to step off a few
paces—say, to a near-by magazine stand—and look at ourselves through the eyes of one of our numerous critics.   If
we do this we shall see that as a class we are 'self-sufficient,
self-deceptive, inadequately educated, greedy, inefficient
and indifferent in cleaning our own house.'   Another critic
begins his article thus: 'In every age the bar has enjoyed
the cynically contemptuous admiration of its contempor-
aries and has been the faithful recipient of the secrets and
confidences of a people that did not trust it.'

*   *   *   *

" 'When it comes to the count of inadequate education I

fear we must plead guilty and throw ourselves upon the tender mercy of democracy. This, and the charge that we have been far too indifferent to house-cleaning, are the really serious counts in the indictment laid against us by our critics.

* * * *

" 'As to education, the matter has two aspects. A sound educational process should take account not merely of technical training in the law but of the development in the student of an entirely new set of instincts.

* * * *

" 'Little by little we can make it clear that formidable educational requirements are in the public interest and that the public interest outweighs the individual interest of the excluded man. Remember, please, that when I speak of educational requirements I always include the element of time and expense of preparation as a deterrent to the commercially-minded youth and those associations during study which stimulate a boy to acquire new instincts. Physicians have an advantage over us in respect to educational reforms. In the same way in war time the Navy has an advantage over the Army. Everybody understands that it requires educational equipment to perform an abdominal operation or to command a battleship. On the other hand, most people imagine that a voluble talker is already a lawyer and that any brave man can command a regiment. Little by little it will be recognized that West Point is no more rigorous than it ought to be and that a law school of the most exacting sort is not an affront to democracy but is necessary to the very life of the Republic.' "

As members of the legal profession it is our duty to the public as well as to ourselves to see that these men who join the ranks are fitted, both from the standpoint of moral character and from the standpoint of general education and legal knowledge, to properly advise and look after their clients' interests. Charles Evans Hughes once said, "The dream that we have, the vision that we have—don't let that fail—of lawyers together feeling that the interests of the profession are not the interests of a minority, but are the interests of all, feeling a duty to establish and maintain standards and willing to discuss with anybody the way to do it, but *intent on getting it done.*"

If we as lawyers will display a solid front in favor of these higher standards there is no doubt that eventually we will achieve them to the everlasting good of the profession and of the public.

The above map shows the minimum amount of general education required of candidates for admission to the bar. Those states which are marked with a numeral have adopted their present requirements in the year indicated. Pennsylvania requires before law study a college degree or passage of a general educational examination independently conducted by the College Board for the State Board of Law Examiners. In Connecticut, Idaho, Minnesota, New Jersey, North Dakota and Rhode Island the full requirements of college education become effective in the future. Washington requires only high school education in case of office students. Massachusetts, Missouri and Nebraska require something less than a four-year high school education.

☐ Two Years Of College Education Or Its Equivalent
▦ High School Or Its Equivalent
■ None

'27

NOTE AND COMMENT

SEARCH FOR AND SEIZURE OF INTOXICATING LIQUORS.—Chapter 36 of the Miss. Code of 1930 contains the state liquor laws and penalties for their violations. This right of the state to punish infractions is not absolute. Oftentimes, it conflicts with the constitutional right of the accused to be free from ''unreasonable search''. Our court has held that if section 23 of the state Constitution, forbidding ''unreasonable search'', is violated evidence secured thereby is inadmissible in court. In not admitting illegally gotten evidence, Mississippi holds with the federal courts and a minority of the state courts. If the state expects to secure convictions for breaches of the liquor laws, it must gain its evidence without violating the constitutional right of the accused to be free from unreasonable searches. Thus, we see it is important to know what are the accused's rights of freedom are in this regard. This discussion will be confined almost entirely to Mississippi law.

Section 23 of our Constitution provides, ''The people shall be secure in their persons, houses, and possessions, from unreasonable seizure or search; and no warrant shall be issued without probable cause, supported by oath or affirmation, specially designating the place to be searched and the person or thing to be seized.'' The interpretation of this section is entirely within the province of the judiciary. It is not within the power of the Legislature to say what is an ''unreasonable seizure or search'' or what is ''probable cause''. The Legislature can provide when a search warrant may be issued and when a search without a warrant may be made so long as the provisions do not conflict with section 23 as interpreted by our Supreme Court.

On proper affidavit that a ''credible person has reason to believe and does believe'' that the liquor law is being violated, section 1975 Code 1930 authorizes issuance of a search warrant commanding search of places or things described. The above statute does not conflict with section 23 of the Constitution guaranteeing that the people shall be secure from ''unreasonable search''. It was contended that this statute was unconstitutional because it allowed the officer no discretion but commanded him to issue a search warrant on the affidavit of any private individual. The court held that the statute enabled the justice to pass judicially on the credibility of the affiant. That interpretation harmonizes with the Constitution. *Winters v. State*, 142 Miss. 71, 107 So. 281.

Section 1976 Code 1930 commands sheriffs, constables, marshals, or policemen in a city to make a reasonable search of vehicles upon reasonable belief that intoxicating liquor is transported therein. This search may be made without a search warrant.

Most of the law of searches and seizures has been created by the judiciary in determining what is a reasonable search. Of course, what would be a reasonable search of an automobile might not be reasonable when applied to a residence, and what would justify search of a residence might not justify search of a man's person. In some of these cases, a search may be made without a warrant, and in others it may not be made at all.

In this article we will consider: (1) search of a person, (2) search of bundles and baggage in the actual possession of a person, (3) requisites of an affidavit, (4) requisites of the search warrant, (5) execution and return of the warrant, and (6) admissibility of the evidence.

Search of a Person

No person can be searched unless first lawfully arrested. We have no statute authorizing the issuance of a warrant for the search of the person of an individual, and the Common Law provides only for the searching of some place or locality. An officer may not search the coat-pocket of an individual by authority of a search warrant. *Comby v. State*, 141 Miss. 561, 106 So. 827; *Duckworth v. Taylorsville*, 142 Miss. 440, 107 So. 666.

In the case of *Daniles v. Gulfport*, 146 Miss. 577, 112 So. 686, the officers heard a disturbance at night and on arriving near the scene threw their light on the defendant. The court held that throwing a light on a person is not an illegal search in the sense that it makes the evidence obtained inadmissible. If the officer sees that a person is committing a crime, he should arrest him and seize the evidence to be used on trial. *Farmer v. State*, 150 Miss. 776, 116 So. 884.

Only after a person is legally arrested can he be searched. An officer lawfully searching a house under a search warrant discovered liquor in the appellant's room. Before arresting her, he searched her dress and found a bottle of liquor concealed there. The court held that the search of her person was illegal because made before arrest. The fact that the arrest could have been made, and that after the arrest a ''reasonable'' search would have been lawful does not affect this case. This case should not be taken to hold that a thorough search of the female would have been ''reasonable'' even if the arrest had been made first. *Robinson v. State*, 143 Miss. 247, 108 So. 903.

Where the arrest was made first, search of the man's person was allowed. *Goodman v. State*, 158 Miss. 269, 130 So. 285. A strong application of this principle, that the arrest must actually be made before a search of a man's person is legal, is found in *Burnside v. State*, 144 Miss. 405, 110 So. 121. In that case, during a lawful search of the premises, an officer saw the wife of the occupant pick up a bottle and put it under her dress. He could not tell whether there was anything in the bottle or not. He had no cause to arrest her and therefore no right to search. When the officer commanded her to give him the whisky, she complied with the order. This was tantamount to an unlawful search of her person and rendered the evidence inadmissible.

Search of Bundles and Baggage in the Actual Possession of a Person.

It is well settled that bundles and baggage in the possession of a person can't be searched unless the officer has a search warrant or unless the person has been lawfully arrested. In the case of *Orick v. State*, 140 Miss. 184, 105 So. 465, an officer went at night to the back of a negro dance-hall to find the cause of a disturbance. When two negroes walked out of the back, he arrested them causing them to drop their jars of liquor. Before the arrest the officer did not know they had any liquor nor did he have any cause to arrest them. The evidence was held to be illegally gained and inadmissible. In a similar case an officer followed a negro down one of the Natchez streets at 4 o'clock A. M. and ordered him to stop. When the negro refused, he fired. The evidence was gained illegally because the officer had neither authority to make the arrest nor any warrant to seize the personal property. Even if the bag was abandoned, the abandonment was caused by the unlawful attempt to arrest. This would render the evidence inadmissible. *Butler v. State*, 133 Miss. 885, 101 So. 193.

If the bailee is in possession, both the bailor and the bailee are protected from unlawful search. Where the owner had turned his suitcase over to a transfer man and the transfer man had set the suitcase down beside him, a marshal searched the suitcase over the protest of the transfer man. Our court held the owner could recover against the marshal for the unlawful search. *U. S. Fidelity & Guaranty Co. v. State*, 121 Miss. 369, 83 So. 610. In the case of *Webb v. State*, 143 Miss. 92, 108 So. 442, the defendant was arrested and the suitcase which he claimed he was carrying for a crippled negro was searched without a warrant. The bag was in the possession of the defendant, and the arrest and search of it was unlawful as to him. Evidence of it was therefore inadmissible in an action against him.

There is no such thing as a right to search baggage in the possession of a person because the officer has a reasonable belief that it contains liquor. Of course if the officer sees the commission of a misdemeanor or has reasonable grounds to suspect that a felony has been committed, he may first arrest the man and then search his person and his baggage. In *Canterberry v. State*, 142 Miss. 462, 107 So. 672, the officer saw the defendant stagger when he dismounted from his horse, and he saw the imprint of a bottle in a jumper folded and tied to the saddle of the defendant's horse. The officer, having no search warrant, searched the bundle and seized the liquor. This was held to be an illegal search because the officer did not know the bundle contained liquor but merely suspected it. The court said, ''We consider packages in the possession of a person, such as suitcases, grips, bundles of wearing apparel, etc., are private possessions which cannot be searched without a warrant, unless the party is first arrested.'' Undoubtedly, if it had been material, the court would have held that the officer had cause to suspect liquor was in the bundle. In the case of *Eady v. State*, 153 Miss. 691, 121 So. 293, the court held that because the officer smelled liquor in a car he had probable cause which justified searching the car without a warrant. No probable cause, in itself, will justify search of bundles in a person's possession.

When a person has been lawfully arrested, both his person and baggage in his possession may be searched. This search is reasonable because the officer should deprive the prisoner of weapons which might aid him to make his escape and because it is the duty of the officer to seize evidence of the crime.

A policeman without a warrant requested a man to let him look in his suitcase, and the man cursed violently in the presence of several persons. The policeman arrested him for profanity. At the police court the man opened his suitcase and told the officer to search if he thought he had any liquor. At no time before the opening of the suitcase was a charge of having liquors preferred against him. This caused a suit against the officer on his bond for unlawful search and unlawful arrest. The lower court found for the defendant on both counts. The Supreme Court affirmed the decision saying that it was not able to say the jury was not warranted in its finding that the plaintiff voluntarily opened his suitcase. In affirming this decision the Supreme Court necessarily held the arrest to be legal. *City of Hattiesburg v. Beverly*, 123 Miss. 759, 86 So. 590. If the arrest was legal, did not the officer have the right to search the suitcase? Why was it necessary to consider whether the plaintiff consented to the search or not? This case does not hold, but it might be taken to imply, that an officer does not have the right, after making a lawful arrest, to search the suitcase which the prisoner is carrying. This right of an officer to search the person's bundle after that person has been lawfully arrested is well settled elsewhere. 240 Fed. 871; 150 S. W. 1177, L. R. A. 1915B 838; 201 N. W. 358, 273 U. S. 782; 206 Pac. 373.

Very few cases occur in which an officer takes out a search warrant to search the baggage in the possession of a person. Of course, if the baggage is not in the possession of the person but is deposited on real property which may be searched, the baggage may be searched as an incident to the search of the real property. See *Sykes v. State*, 157 Miss. 600, 128 So. 753 for a case where the personal property deposited on the real property was particularly pointed out to be searched.

In the case of *Bates v. State*, 143 Miss. 772, 109 So. 730, the officers had a valid search warrant for the house in which the defendant was. During the search they took from the defendant's hands a sack which contained two cold bottles of liquor. The imprint in the ice showed they were taken from the refrigerator. The bundle, being private personal property in the individual's possession and being searched without a warrant, was rendered inadmissible in evidence. Thus, we see that the person is protected in the possession of bundles even though he is on property which is being lawfully searched. The court might have decided this case on the fact that even after objection of the defendant the state failed to produce the affidavit on which the search warrant was based, and failed to account for its absence. This, of itself, rendered the evidence inadmissible.

A real difficulty appears in trying to determine whether a warrant may be gotten for the search of baggage which a person is carrying about with him. If he cannot be lawfully arrested, this question is of importance, because we have already seen that his baggage, in such a case, may not be searched offhand. There are few cases involving this question. There is no Mississippi authority on this point. Dicta in several of the cases might be taken to imply that search by search warrant is permissible. *Bates v. State*, 143 Miss. 772, 109 So. 730; *Canterberry v. State*, 142 Miss. 462, 107 So. 672. A question might arise as to whether this would be in conflict with Section 23 of the State Constitution which prohibits ''unreasonable'' searches and requires that a search warrant especially designates the ''place'' to be searched. See *State v. Fezette*, 103 Me. 467, 69 Atl. 1073, quoted in *Robinson v. State*, 143 Miss. 247, 108 So. 903. Also 2 JJ Marsh (Ky.) 44; and 203 Mass. 516, 89 N. E. 1046.

It must be remembered that one who is neither the owner nor the possessor of property can not object to unlawful search of it. The defendant, disclaiming ownership and possession of a suitcase containing liquor, may not complain of the testimony of an officer based on unlawful search thereof. *Ross v. State*, 140 Miss. 367, 105 So. 847. Same as to abandoned property, but the abandonment must not be caused by unlawful pursuit of the law. *Butler v. State*, 135 Miss. 885, 101 So. 193.

Requisites of an Affidavit.

FORM AND CONTENTS:

The form of the affidavit set out in Section 1977 Code 1930 may be used. It is merely permissible, but Section 1975, as to when an affidavit is to be used and what it must contain, is mandatory.

Section 1975 Code 1930 is mandatory and the affiant must swear both ''that he has reason to believe and does believe,'' and unless he does, the search warrant is void. *Turner v. State,* 133 Miss. 738, 98 So. 249; *State v. Watson,* 133 Miss. 796, 98 So. 241; *Porter v. State,* 135 Miss. 789, 100 So. 377. However, where the affiant charges absolute knowledge of the facts, that is sufficient. *Kelley v. State,* 131 So. 272.

It is not error to allege disjunctively the grounds for a search warrant as it is in the case of an attachment because, in attachment according to some writers, it is necessary to tell which ground is relied on in order that pleas in abatement may be filed. This reason can have no particular force when applied to an affidavit for the issuance of a search warrant. Also, the statute allows joining the grounds disjunctively. *Banks v. City of Jackson,* 152 Miss. 844, 120 So. 209.

The fact that the affidavit was dated the day after the search warrant did not make it necessary to amend the affidavit before introducing the search warrant because issuing of the search warrant was a judicial finding that the affidavit was proper. The evidence showed the search warrant was based on the affidavit and the dating was a mere oversight. *Hendricks v. State,* 144 Miss. 87, 109 So. 263.

Note the difference in 2338 Hemingway's Code of 1927, and 1975 Code 1930 as to the requirements under sub-section 1 as to what is necessary for the affiant to swear. It is not necessary any longer to swear that the liquor was possessed ''for the purpose of sale in violation of law.'' Because of the change, *Estes v. State,* 152 Miss. 555, 120 So. 444, is no longer law.

Since the description of the place to be searched in an affidavit is similar to the description of the place to be searched in the search warrant, both subjects are considered under Requisites of the Search Warrant in the division on Description of Place to Be Searched.

VERIFICATION:

The recital in the affidavit that the oath was taken, will not be overturned by the uncertain testimony of the affiant that he was doubtful but his best recollection was he did not take the oath. *Borders v. State,* 138 Miss. 788, 104 So. 145. See *Atwood v. State,* 146 Miss. 662, 111 So. 865 for a good discussion of the requisites of an oath. It holds that the affiant need not go through any formal statement. If he and the officer intend what they do to amount to the taking of an oath, that is sufficient. An affidavit may be good even though the affiant does not sign it. Section 4, c. 244 of the laws of 1924 (similar to section 1977 Code 1930) is directory and not mandatory and therefore does not command that the affiant sign the affidavit. *Winters v. State,* 142 Miss. 71, 107 So. 281.

In making out the affidavit, by mistake of the officer, the wrong name was written for the party whose house was to be searched. After the search, the affiant said the officer had written the wrong name in the affidavit and in the search warrant, and that the defendant's house was the house which ought to have been searched. The agreement of facts shows that the name in the search warrant was changed but it does not mention the affidavit. The defendant's house was searched and the liquor was found. These facts do not amount to an oath to authorize the issuance of the altered search warrant. *Gizzard v. State*, 149 Miss. 323, 115 So. 555. This case does not come within that of *Atwood v. State, supra,* because the affiant did no act which would constitute the making of an oath to an affidavit authorizing the issuance of a search warrant for the defendant's premises.

Requisites of a Search Warrant.

A search warrant must be based on a good affidavit. A warrant issued on a defective affidavit is illegal. *State v. Watson,* 133 Miss. 796, 98 So. 241. A justice may issue a warrant to any part of his county on proper affidavit. *Buffin v. State,* 134 Miss. 1, 98 So. 452; *Goffredo v. State,* 145 Miss. 66, 111 So. 131. Usually, the mayor is an ex-officio justice of the peace and may issue a search warrant to any part of his county. *Falkner v. State,* 134 Miss. 101, 98 So. 345. But an affidavit taken and a search warrant issued by the mayor of a city having a police justice under 6943 Hem. Code. 1917 (Sec. 2536 Code 1930) is void because the mayor has no function as ex-officio justice of the peace. *Palmer v. City of Lumberton,* 153 Miss. 886, 122 So. 199. A city clerk can't issue a search warrant. 135 Miss. 789, 100 So. 377. Failure to name the district of the justice issuing the affidavit does not invalidate a search warrant which names county and state because the justice has the power to issue a warrant to any part of his county. 152 Miss. 154, 118 So. 719.

Under Section 2088 Hem. Code (similar to Sec. 1975 Code 1930) authorizing a search warrant to be issued to the sheriff or any constable or marshal, a warrant directed "to any lawful officer of said county" is not void where the justice delivered it to the sheriff to be executed by him. *Matthews v. State,* 134 Miss. 807, 100 So. 18. Section 2919 Hem. Code (Sec. 2964 Code 1930), saying that all process except where otherwise provided shall be issued by the clerk of the court with the seal of his office attached, has no application to process issued by a justice because he is not required by law to have a seal. *Matthews v. State, supra.*

Necessity of a Search Warrant.

Land can't be searched without a search warrant unless the rightful possessor consents. *Helton v. State,* 101 So. 701, 136 Miss. 622. The wooded lands of Tom Falkner were searched by officers without a warrant, and liquor was found 300 yards from his residence. The court held that the search was illegal as to him because Section 23 of the Constitution prohibits unreasonable searches of any property. *Falkner v. State,* 134 Miss. 253, 98 So. 691. Some courts consider that a search of unenclosed lands without a search warrant is not unreasonable, but our court tends toward giving the fullest protection against searches and seizures.

The lessee of land is given the same protection which the owner, if he were in possession, would be awarded. The "possessions" protected in Section 23 of the Constitution extend to unenclosed lands of the lessee. *Bernard v. State,* 155 Miss. 390, 124 So. 479. Even though the occupant of the premises pays no rent but holds with the permission of the owner, he is protected from a search without a warrant. *Davis v. State,* 144 Miss. 551, 110 So. 447. The defendant can complain of an illegal search of the home place occupied by him and his wife even if the title is in his wife. *Sanders v. State,* 141 Miss. 615, 106 So. 822. And the wife can complain of an illegal search of her husband's house. *Brewer v. State,* 142 Miss. 100, 107 So. 376. However, the son living away from home can't complain of an illegal search of his father's house. *Roberts v. State,* 153 Miss. 622, 121 So. 279.

There are at least four situations when evidence obtained from search of land and buildings is admissible even though there was no search warrant: (A) When the defendant is not the rightful possessor of the land searched; (B) When land is searched with the defendant's consent; (C) When a private person makes the search; and, (D) When an officer goes on the land to make a legal arrest.

The defendant can't avail himself of the unlawful search unless he is the owner or rightful possessor of the property violated. The defendant in *Falkner v. State, supra,* who was not the owner or rightful possessor of the land illegally searched, could not take advantage of the owner's defense. Other cases upholding this principle are *Lee v. Oxford,* 134 Miss. 647, 99 So. 509; *Webb v. State,* 143 Miss. 92, 108 So. 442; *Messer v. State,* 107 So. 384, not off. rep.; *Loven v. State,* 140 Miss. 635, 105 So. 759.

When the defendant consents to a search of his premises, he can't object to the introduction of the still found during the search. *Faulk v. State,* 127 Miss. 894, 90 So. 481. The waiver of the search warrant must be clearly expressed; or the court, taking into consideration the situation of the parties, will not regard it. Where the officer, beginning the search without a search warrant, said he was going to search, and the defendant said, "All right, you are welcome if you can find it," our court has held that there was no waiver of the search warrant. *Smith v. State,* 133 Miss. 730, 98 So. 344.

Evidence gained by illegal search of a private person is admissible. Section 23 of the Constitution forbidding unreasonable search has no application to search by authorized acts of private persons. *Hampton v. State,* 132 Miss. 154, 96 So. 165. A town marshal without a search warrant and acting under color of authority searched a car four miles out of town. The court held he could not testify as to what he found because the evidence was illegally obtained. An officer acting under color of authority does not stand on the same footing with a private individual. *State v. Messer,* 142 Miss. 882, 108 So. 145.

If an illegal search is made by a federal officer, the evidence is not admissible in federal court. However, if they did not act in conjunction with state officers, the evidence might be used in our state courts. The law says that the federal officers stand on the same footing in this respect as private citizens. The reason is that the guarantee of the State Constitution is made to protect against the encroachments of the state government and not the federal government. It is also true, that when a state official, acting independently of the federal officers, makes an unlawful search, the evidence gained thereby is admissible in federal court. *Weeks v. U. S.,* 232 U. S. 383, 34 Sup Ct. 341. Of course the officer, be he state or federal officer, is liable in a civil suit for the illegal search. If we lived under only one government, we would have full protection against the illegal searches of its officials, but since we are under two governments, we have no certain protection from the officials of either.

It must be remembered that any premises can be invaded without a warrant to search for an offender when the officer goes to make a legal arrest. *Kennedy v. State*, 139 Miss. 579, 104 So. 449. A sheriff may go on the land to make an arrest when informed by a credible person that a felony is being committed. *Ingram v. State*, 146 Miss. 303, 111 So. 362. In the case above, *Kennedy v. State*, the officer on the information of a credible person, went on the premises to seize a still. The evidence procured was admissible on trial. Even though the arrest is prevented by flight, the officer may testify as to still he saw. *Wallace v. State*, 149 Miss. 639.

An officer, having a warrant for the arrest of a felon but no search warrant, and having reliable information that the felon was at another's house, has a right to make a reasonable search of the house for the felon. *Monette v. Toney*, 119 Miss. 846, 81 So. 593. Of course, if while searching for the felon, the officer finds intoxicating liquor, he has the right to seize it.

After the arrest has been made, the officer has a duty to search the place to get evidence of the crime committed. Dictum in *King v. State*, 147 Miss. 31, 113 So. 173, says the right of search after a lawful arrest is not so great as that under a search warrant.

There is one other important situation when a search may be made without a warrant. An officer may search a vehicle or boat when he has reason to believe and does believe that it is being used to violate the liquor laws. This is not an unreasonable search within the meaning of Section 23 of the Constitution. "The impracticability in most cases of obtaining a warrant for the search of swift moving vehicles and boats before they can be moved beyond reach justifies the distinction made between them and dwelling houses and similar places and renders a search of vehicles and boats without a warrant reasonable." Reasonable belief may be founded on facts given by a credible person. *Moore v. State*, 138 Miss. 116, 103 So. 483; *Brown v. State*, 149 Miss. 219, 115 So. 436.

An officer, having no information about the defendant with reference to crime and searching the defendant's car without a warrant and without probable cause, acts illegally and the defendant can't be convicted on evidence obtained thereby. *Cook v. State*, 111 So. 381, not off. rep. Ninety days before the night the defendant's auto was searched, Moore had told the officer that he (Moore) had bought whisky from the defendant and that was the reason the defendant would have whisky whenever he came to Belzoni about 12 o'clock at night. There was no probable cause for the search 90 days after this speculative statement. *Gardner v. State*, 145 Miss. 210, 110 So. 588.

The marshal "balled" the defendant and his companions out for running without a muffler, and told them to come back and pay a fine next day. Upon smelling liquor on their breath, he searched the car and found four gallons of whisky. Though the officer had the authority to make an arrest, telling them to come back next day did not amount to an arrest. Smelling liquor on their breaths did not amount to probable cause to search the car. The evidence was illegally obtained. *Chrestman v. State*, 148 Miss. 673, 114 So. 748.

In the case of *King v. State*, 152 Miss. 580, 118 So. 413, the officers had information that C had liquor and that people were going to his house for it. They stopped the defendant about one mile from C's house and were going to let him by until they saw Mc in the car with him. The sheriff admitted he had no reason to suspect the defendant until he saw Mc with him. The search was without reasonable cause, and the evidence therefore inadmissible.

Late one night the plaintiff was driving zigzag down the streets of Laurel, and the occupants of his car were laughing and talking loud. When they stopped to look at the tires, the officers drove their car in front of the plaintiff's and made a search of the plaintiff's car. Plaintiff brought action for the unlawful search against the two policemen and their sureties. The court held that there was no probable cause for the search and that the defendants were liable. *Sellers et al. v. Lofton*, 149 Miss. 849, 116 So. 104.

It is often difficult to determine whether there is probable cause to justify an officer searching a car without a warrant. The following situations have been held to justify search of a car without a search warrant: when the officer smelled whisky on the breath of an occupant of the car and saw a bottle of liquor lying on the back seat (*Arnold v. State*, 153 Miss. 299, 120 So. 731); when the officers, in lawfully searching for another car, flashed a light on the defendant as the defendant's car slowed down to pass the officer, and one of the occupants ran from the car, and the defendant on being asked admitted he had liquor in his car (*Williamson v. State*, 105 So. 479, 140 Miss. 841); when the officer smelled liquor, not on the breath of the occupants, but in the car (*Eady v. State*, 153 Miss. 691, 121 So. 293); and when the sheriff communicated the information to the police that the defendant would be delivering liquor in a certain car in the negro quarters on Sunday morning (*Story v. City of Greenwood*, 153 Miss. 755, 121 So. 481).

In the last named case the court held that it was immaterial as to where the sheriff got his information because it was given in a positive nature and the policemen had a right to rely on him. But in a case where a deputy sheriff gets his information from his sheriff, even though a reasonable man would believe it, probable cause can not be determined from the deputy's viewpoint. The raid would be under the direction of the sheriff, and therefore it would be his raid. The question of probable cause must be determined from the sheriff's viewpoint—whether the sheriff had a reasonable belief that the law was being violated. *Smith v. State*, 160 Miss. 46, 133 So. 240.

It is easy to tell that the evidence in some cases does not constitute "probable cause" for a search without a warrant, but it is difficult to tell just what is required to constitute "probable cause" justifying an officer searching a vehicle without a warrant. In the late case of *Elardo v. State*, ... Miss. ...., 145 So. 615, the deputy sheriff was told by the informer that he (the informer) had information that a truck load of liquor was stuck at a certain place and that the truck was driven by H's son-in-law. The informer did not tell the nature of his information. The search was made. Our Supreme Court held there was no "probable cause" justifying search without a warrant. The requirements for "probable cause" set forth in the case are: (1) the information must be communicated as a fact within the knowledge of the informant; (2) the information must be evidence such as would be competent on the trial of the offense before a jury; and (3) it must be such as would lead a man of prudence and caution to believe the offense has been committed.

The above case says that "probable cause" sufficient to allow search without a search warrant is sufficient to justify the issuing of a warrant. "The right to make a search without a warrant is never greater than it would be to obtain a warrant." The third requisite set forth in *Elardo v. State* is well settled and has been dealt with in the previous cases of this division. The first and second requirements are not definitely settled. The court probably means by the first requirement that the informant must have personal knowledge of the commission of the crime. However, it is possible that it means that the informant must state the facts he knows, and that stating the source of his hearsay testimony is the stating of a fact within his knowledge. It should be noted that the source of the hearsay information was not stated in the case of *Elardo v. State, supra.*

Loeb v. State, 133 Miss. 883, 98 So. 449, held that "probable cause in law is a charge of crime made on oath, without regard to the fact whether the oath is made on personal knowledge or upon information and belief merely. . . . The legislature did not intend the affidavit to be made on personal knowledge." The court did not say, and it is not easy to determine, whether *Elardo v. State* overrulled this part of *Loeb v. State* or not. It is possible to reconcile the cases if we conclude that *Elardo v. State* decided only that the informant stating he had been informed, without stating the facts as to how he had gotten his information, does not give "probable cause" to search a car. Then this would allow, in accord with *Loeb v. State,* the informer to make the charge on information and belief, without stating the commission of the crime as a fact, if he tells the source of his hearsay information, and if the whole is sufficient to make a reasonably prudent man believe the crime has been committed.

In the *Elardo case, supra,* the state cited *Story v. City of Greenwood,* 153 Miss. 755, 121 So. 481, but the court held that this was not in point because the informant stated his information as a fact within his knowledge. In *Story v. Greenwood* the informant told the officer the defendant would be delivering whisky in the negro quarters of Greenwood early Sunday morning in a Dodge automobile. Something predicted to happen in the future is not a fact. It is an opinion. So far as the reported case shows, the informant did not state the facts on which he based his opinion. A bald prediction cannot be mistaken for a statement of fact. It is not evidence which would be admissible in court. In the *Story case,* we have an opinion unsupported by facts; in the *Elardo case,* hearsay information was given without stating the source of the information. It is difficult to see how the evidence in the *Story case* can be considered "probable cause"; and, at the same time the evidence in *Elardo v. State* insufficient. By not sufficiently disposing of the *Loeb* and the *Story* cases, the court left the law on this point in an unsettled state.

We can reconcile *Elardo v. State, supra,* with the previous Mississippi cases on this question of "probable cause" only by adopting a strained construction. It is better to conclude that this is a change in the law which has come about since Prohibition has fallen into disfavor. The courts, reflecting the change in public sentiment, are looking more closely into the cases to see whether the accused's constitutional rights of freedom from "unreasonable searches" have been violated. In the *Elardo case* our court interpreted our state statute in the light of the federal statute and thereby incorporated into our law the first and second requirement of "probable cause" set forth in *Elardo v. State, supra.*

In the case of *Ford v. City of Jackson,* 153 Miss. 616, 121 So. 278, the policemen said that they had information that the defendant was selling liquor on certain streets. They pursued his car in theirs. The defendant threw a bottle of liquor out of his car. The policemen got it, overtook him, and found eight pints of whisky in the car. Over objection this evidence was admitted. The lower court held that, after the defendant had asked for the source of the information, it was not necessary for the officers to state the source of their information. The Supreme Court held that the defendant was entitled to know the source of the officers' information with a view of challenging its sufficiency as well as the credibility of the officers claiming to have had probable cause to search. Since no probable cause was shown for beginning the search, and since the bottle of liquor as well as the eight pints were gained after illegal pursuit had begun, evidence of the liquor was inadmissible.

On information given by the manager of H. G. plantation and a doctor that liquor had been stored in a cotton-house on H. G. plantation, the deputies hid near the cotton-house. One of the deputies looked into the cotton-house and saw the cans of liquor, but neither of the officers knew the contents of the cans till after arrest. The defendant and another drove up and took three cans of liquor out of the house and put one of them in the car. They were arrested and afterwards searched. The court held that there was probable cause for the search and the fact that incident to it the defendant was arrested did not render the evidence found during the search inadmissible. *Holmes v. State*, 146 Miss. 351, 111 So. 860. The arrest alone was not justified because the misdemeanor was not committed in the officer's ''presence'' in the sense that in the ''presence'' is used in Section 1227 Code 1930 which action gives the officer the right to arrest for misdemeanors. The officer must be aware of all the elements of the misdemeanor from knowledge gained through his own senses.

If he can be granted that there was no ground for arrest, this case is similar to *Carroll v. U. S.*, 267 U. S. 132, 45 Sup. Ct. 280. In that case the officers had the right to search the car but did not have the right to arrest. As is pointed out in 24 Columbia Law Review 277, the majority opinion treats the case as though the officers made the search, they were legally entitled to make, and then arrested the defendants after the liquor had been discovered. The dissenting judge considers the arrest as made first, when there was no legal right to arrest, only the right to search. Therefore, the dissenting judge found no trouble in declaring the evidence gained under the illegal arrest inadmissible. The author of the Law Review article above said: ''The position of the majority would oblige them to concede that if the arrest had preceded the search the defendants would have at least a technical right to recover damages for the illegal arrest, even though the subsequent search be held valid.'' Even if the arrest be illegally made the subsequent search should not thereby be rendered illegal because the officers did have a right to search before the arrest was made.

In the Mississippi case, *Holmes v. State, supra*, the court gracefully hurdled the difficulty by saying the arrest was ''incident'' to the arrest. This enabled the court to avoid undue refinement of the law.

The officer arresting a person having control of a car may search the car. In the case of *Toliver v. State*, 133 Miss. 789, 98 So. 342, a sheriff had a warrant for the arrest of Toliver for selling a truck on which there was a lien. The sheriff meeting Toliver in a car on the road arrested him and found the liquor in a sack in an open box on the back seat. It was admitted that upon arrest the officer has the right to search the person and take things which might be helpful in aiding the prisoner to escape. This reason and the fact that the officer could not leave the car on the road justified his examining and taking possession of the car.

Taylor v. State, 129 Miss. 815, 93 So. 355, from a reading of the court's opinion seems contra to the above case. In *Taylor v. State* the appellant was arrested and his buggy searched. The evidence found in the buggy was held inadmissible. The opinion does not say but the briefs in the Mississippi Reports show that the arrest was illegally made. Granting this, the cases are not conflicting.

Of course, as has been said before in the case of searches of land, an unauthorized search by an individual does not make the evidence obtained inadmissible against the owner of rightful possessor. But an officer outside his jurisdiction, acting under color of office does not stand on the same footing as an individual in this regard. In the case of *State v. Messer*, 142 Miss. 882, 108 So. 145, the town marshal and a private citizen without a search warrant searched a car four miles out of town and found liquor. Though the officer could not do official acts there, his acts were under color of office, and the evidence has the same infirmity as if he had been performing an official act. The point was not raised, but the private citizen whom the officer asked to go with him can't testify either. As to the qualifications on his testimony, he stands on the same ground as the officer himself.

PROBABLE CAUSE:

In *Loeb v. State*, 133 Miss. 883, 98 So. 449, the defendant contended that Section 2088 Hem. Code (Section 1975 Code 1930) was unconstitutional because, he maintained, it commanded the justice, without any discretion on his part, to issue a search warrant upon the affidavit of any credible person that he had reason to believe and did believe that the liquor law was being violated. The court held that this statute allowed the justice to pass on the credibility of the witness and it was therefore within the Constitution. The issuance of a search warrant is an adjudication that there is "probable cause" to search.

The same case. says that the affiant is not required to have personal knowledge of the facts stated in the affidavit and that an affidavit based on information and belief is sufficient. In the late case of *Elardo v. State*, ... Miss. ...., 145 So. 615, there are some disturbing dicta concerning search warrants. In considering what "probable cause" justified search of a car without a search warrant the court considered what "probable cause" justified the issuance of a search warrant. The court said, "The information must be communicated as a fact within the knowledge of the person communicating the information. . . . A search warrant may issue only upon evidence which would be competent in the trial of the offense before a jury." This is of importance in the federal courts because, according to federal law, the judge's determination of "probable cause" for the issuance may be inquired into. It is unimportant in our state law because, after a judge has issued a search warrant and thereby found "probable cause" to exist, it is conclusive as between the defendant and the state. In *Mai v. State* the court said, ". . . To permit the defendant to challenge the truth of the judicial finding of the officer issuing the warrant that probable cause existed therefor would open up for trial an issue collateral to that of the guilt or innocence of the defendant. . . . The field of inquiry . . . would be calculated to divert the minds of the jury from the main issue." It is submitted that the determination of whether "probable cause" existed for the issuance of a search warrant could be left up to the judge, just as it is when it is claimed that an officer, without a warrant has searched a car when he had no probable cause to search. However, the law is well settled that the judge's issuance of a search warrant is a conclusive determination of "probable cause" for the issuance thereof.

Thus, it would seem that if an officer who did not have "probable cause" to search a car went before a justice of the peace and made an affidavit, and if the justice issued a search warrant, the justice's finding of probable cause would be conclusive. The officer could take the search warrant and make a legal search of the car. By this procedural method the accused is deprived of his constitutional right to be free from unreasonable search. Our Constitution guarantees us freedom from unreasonable searches yet it is held that a justice of the peace, a man usually unlearned in the law, can take away this constitutional right and there is no appeal from his decision. No one can doubt but that this is a legal atrocity.

DESCRIPTION OF THE PROPERTY TO BE SEIZED:

Loeb v. State, 133 Miss. 883, 98 So. 449, holds that it is sufficient to describe the intoxicating liquors to be seized simply as intoxicating liquors because it is not probable that a person will know the exact nature of the liquors.

The officers had a lawful warrant to search the defendant's premises for intoxicating liquor and during the search found shot-gun shells. In a trial for murder the shells were used against the defendant over his objection. The evidence was not admissible because the search warrant was for intoxicating liquors, and the possession of the shells was not unlawful per se. *Cofer v. State,* 152 Miss. 761, 118 So. 613. This case is to be distinguished from *Reynolds v. State,* 136 Miss. 329, 101 So. 485, in which the officers seized a still under a search warrant for intoxicating liquors. · In both cases the officers were lawfully on the premises. In the latter case the possession of the still was unlawful per se; in the former the possession of the shells was not.

DESCRIPTION OF PLACE:

Section 23 of the Miss. Constitution says that, "no warrant shall be issued without probable cause, supported by oath or affirmation, specially designating the place to be searched and the person or thing to be seized." Section 1975 Code 1930, providing for the making of the affidavit and issuance of the search warrant, commands the search of the place described in the affidavit. Since the description in the affidavit and search warrant should be the same, the requirements of the description in the search warrant and in the affidavit may be considered together.

In the case of *Rignall v. State,* 134 Miss. 169, 98 So. 444, the only description in the warrant was to "search the premises of Joe Rignall." The word premises has varying meanings, and a warrant to search the "premises" without other description or limitation as to occupancy or use and without any designation of county is too broad to be good. This defect was cured where, the state and county having been named, the place was described as "the premises occupied by L. A. Matters in district No. 5 about 14 miles northeast of Hazlehurst in said county and state." *Matthews v. State,* 134 Miss. 807, 100 So. 18. Also see *Borders v. State,* 138 Miss. 788, 104 So. 145.

A sheriff made an affidavit which described the place to be searched as the premises of W. M. Parkinson estate about 7 miles east of Cruger in said state and county and the warrant declared it was not feigned of malice to said W. M. Parkinson. This was not good because it described the place to be searched as the premises of a deceased person. *George Parkinson v. State*, 145 Miss. 237, 110 So. 513.

Generally, the description of the place to be searched is sufficient if it enables the officer to locate the premises definitely. "A description may be one used in the locality and known to the people, if it is sufficiently suggestive that an officer by reasonable inquiry may locate with certainty the place to be searched." A description such as, "a certain room or building and all out-houses occupied by James or Zeke Bradley situated in Forest County, Mississippi" is sufficient. *Bradley v. State*, 134 Miss. 20, 98 So. 458.

In the case of *Forshee v. State*, 152 Miss. 566, 120 So. 462, the warrant for the search of the defendant's dwelling house described the place to be searched as "the dwelling house and premises, including all barns, outhouses, where the said John Forshee now lives, and which said buildings now occupied and used by him, the said John Forshee, including the place, yards, and curtilage thereof." The house was erroneously described as being "on the Bob Box Farm, or near the Bob Box house, near Big Black river, in Choctaw County, State of Mississippi." The home of the appellant, Forshee, is about a mile and a half from the Box Farm. This fact does not avoid the description for it is clear that the place to be searched was the dwelling house and the premises in Choctaw County on and in which the appellant then lived. The further description that it was on or near the Bob Box farm may be treated as surplusage, there being no contention that the defendant had more than one residence. *Forshee v. State*, 152 Miss. 566, 120 So. 462.

The street address is sufficient. An affidavit describing the place to be searched as "a building occupied by Susie Loeb at a residence on Thirty Third avenue, House No. 1009 in the city of Meridian, Miss." is good. *Loeb v. State*, 133 Miss. 883, 98 So. 449. An affidavit which describes the place to be searched as "the dwelling house, outhouses, in the automobile or other vehicles used or occupied by and on the person of Unknown occupant at 123 West Griffith Street in the city of Jackson in said county and state," has sufficiently described the place to be searched. *Banks v. City of Jackson*, 152 Miss. 844, 120 So. 209.

Several cases have reached our Supreme Court in which the officers have attempted to use a blank search warrant so that they might search around first and fill in the warrant later. Where the search was made with a search warrant based upon an affidavit which left the description of the place out (evidently intending to fill it in later), the search was illegal and the evidence inadmissible. *Spears v. State*, 99 So. 361, not off. rep. Writing in the name of the place to be searched after the liquor has been found is not good. *Miller v. State*, 129 Miss. 774, 93 So. 2. A warrant to search the premises of "John Doe" is void. *Brewer v. State*, 142 Miss. 100, 107 So. 376. If such warrants as these were allowed, it would give unlimited authority to search.

A valid search warrant to search a certain place does not give the right to search the adjoining property. A search warrant described the place to be searched as "a certain room in a building occupied by T. Strangi." No liquor was found there, but liquor was found in another building 100 feet away from the place described. The search was held illegal and the evidence inadmissible. *Strangi v. State*, 134 Miss. 31, 98 So. 340. A search warrant to search one place, however good it may be, cannot be used to search another. *Owens v. State*, 133 Miss. 753, 98 So. 233. Under a search warrant for the search of a "certain room in a building occupied by Nick Fatimo," no liquor was found in the room, but liquor was found in the back yard under an old counter some distance from the house. The search in this case was declared illegal. *Fatimo v. State*, 134 Miss. 175, 98 So. 537.

In Mississippi a warrant must be secured to search unenclosed lands. When deputies have a warrant to search the premises and they search a cane brake too, evidence secured by search of the brake is not admissible against the lessor. *Barnard v. State*, 155 Miss. 390, 124 Co. 479.

A sheriff got a warrant to search C's car and under it searched V's car in which C was riding. The search was illegal because the search warrant did not describe the place to be searched as V's car. *Vaughn v. State*, 136 Miss. 314, 101 So. 439.

In the case of *Carnaggio v. State*, 143 Miss. 694, 109 So. 732, the officer who aided in the search made an affidavit describing the car to be searched as an automobile in the possession of, and driven by John Carnaggio, within the city of Lexington, Miss. The search by search warrant of the car outside the city limits was held valid by our Supreme Court. As the search warrant was to search the car and not the person, the description was too indefinite. It was a warrant to search any car Carnaggio might have been in possession of when he was found.

Execution and Return of the Warrant.

See Section 1975 as to the duty of an officer to execute a proper warrant. A failure to serve the search warrant which the officers have does not affect the search when they ask permission to search and the defendant tells them to help themselves. If the defendant had objected, the officers could have shown their search warrant. *Forshee v. State*, 152 Miss. 566, 120 So. 462.

A search warrant addressed "to any lawful officer of Forest County, Mississippi" was served by a policeman within the city. The defendant contends that policemen are not lawful officers of the county. Section 2241 Hem. Code 1927 (Section 1978 Code 1930) says the warrant is to be addressed "to any lawful officer of (said) county." Section 2238 Hem. Code 1927 (Section 1975 Code 1930) says the warrant may be directed to the sheriff or any constable or marshal or policeman in a municipality commanding him to search the place described. Section 3148 Hem. Code 1927 (Section 2990 Code 1930) says that any process appearing to be in other respects duly served shall be good, though not directed to any officer. Therefore, the process was lawfully directed and lawfully executed. *Keys v. State*, 155 Miss. 574, 124 So. 789. If a policeman serves the warrant, he must not serve it outside the city. *State v. Messer*, 142 Miss. 882, 108 So. 145.

Under the old law, Section 2088 Hem. Code, the search warrant for intoxicating liquors was required to be returnable on a day not earlier than five days after its issuance. But if it was returnable earlier, it was valid if it did not prejudice the rights of the defendant. *Buffin v. State*, 98 So. 452, 134 Miss. 1. The above code section was amended by Laws 1924, c. 244, section

1, so that a warrant is required to be "returnable instanter or a day stated" and a copy served on the possessor if he be readily found. The warrant should be returnable within a reasonable time; and if it is returnable to a past date, it is void. *Buckley v. State*, 150 Miss. 808, 117 So. 115; *McSwain v. State*, 158 Miss. 643, 130 So. 696.

Powell v. State, 146 Miss. 677, 111 So. 738, holds that a search warrant with no return date is invalid because it evades the direct command of the statute and leaves it open to abuse. Where a search warrant is made returnable to a past date, evidence procured by it is inadmissible. *McSwain v. State*, 158 Miss. 643, 130 So. 696. A search warrant should be returnable before the justice of the district in which the search is made, but a return before another justice will not avoid it. *Reynolds v. State*, 136 Miss. 329, 101 So. 485. "The warrant is not void because an improper return is made thereon. It is amendable in the court to which it is returnable, and may be changed to conform to the facts." *Washington v. State*, 152 Miss. 154, 118 So. 719.

Admissibility of the Evidence.

When an illegal search has been made and a constitutional right violated; the person making the search is liable in a civil suit to the injured party. The question of illegal search comes up when the party being prosecuted for a crime objects to the introduction of evidence discovered by an officer during an illegal search. In such a case, the defendant has a right to have all the evidence illegally gained excluded from the jury.

It is proper for the court to refuse to hear and pass upon a motion to suppress evidence illegally gained before the beginning of the trial and before the evidence was offered. When the evidence is offered and proper objection is interposed it then becomes the duty of the trial judge to pass upon and decide the question of its competency. Where the defendant does not request the preliminary examination to be made in the absence of the jury, he will be held to have waived his right. It is the duty of the trial judge to hear the facts and determine whether the evidence is admissible. *Holmes v. State*, 146 Miss. 351, 111 So. 860; *Holley v. State*, 144 Miss. 726, 111 So. 139; *McNutt v. State*, 143 Miss. 347, 108 So. 721. What has been said in this paragraph applies when the State is attempting to use ill gained evidence to convict the defendant of a crime; it does not apply when the person searched is bringing suit against the officer. In the latter case the determination of whether there was "probable cause" is a question for the jury. *McNutt v. State*, 143 Miss. 347, 108 So. 721.

It necessarily follows from the rule, that illegally gotten evidence is inadmissible, that, when the search under which the evidence was obtained required a search warrant, the affidavit and search warrant must be produced or their absence accounted for on trial, if the defendant objects to the evidence. *Cuevas v. Gulfport*, 134 Miss. 644, 99 So. 503; *Wells v. State*, 135 Miss. 764, 100 So. 674. If this were not so there would be no way of testing the validity of the search and the legality of the evidence.

For the same reason, the officer who searches a car on information given by a "credible man" must give that man's name when asked for it in court. Only after obtaining the information is the accused able to contradict the officer and test the credibility of the information. *Hamilton v. State*, 149

Miss. 251, 115 So. 427. When the officer has shown the source of the information which he deemed credible, it is for the court to determine the credibleness of the information.

Oftentimes, when liquor is found by illegal search in the possession of the accused, he confesses to the crime for which he is afterwards tried. The corpus delicti of the crime can't be established by the confession of the accused alone, and the illegally gotten evidence is inadmissible. The defendant was arrested and carried to his place where the officers without a search warrant discovered a still. The defendant confessed that he had been engaged in making liquor. The evidence obtained from the search was inadmissible, and the confession alone was not sufficient to establish the corpus delicti. The court should have directed a verdict of not guilty. *Williams v. State*, 129 Miss. 469, 92 So. 584. But after the corpus delicti is established by legally gotten evidence a confession or plea of guilty in a former trial is admissible. *Sykes v. State*, 157 Miss. 600, 128 So. 753.

The accused cannot complain regarding admission of evidence obtained by unlawful search and seizure, if he testifies to facts revealed by such evidence. Where the accused's car was searched on information which may not have amounted to probable cause—though the court did not pass upon it—and he testified to the possession of the liquor, it was immaterial whether the evidence was illegally gotten or not. *Bowman v. State*, 152 Miss. 195, 119 So. 176. But if the accused objects to the evidence and does not admit the facts discovered by the illegal search, it is improper to admit the evidence on trial. *Barnard v. State*, 155 Miss. 390, 124 So. 479.

In *Nicaise v. State*, 141 Miss. 611, 106 So. 817, the officers searched the defendant's home without a search warrant and found a still. He was indicted for possessing a still used for the manufacture of intoxicating liquor. The officers testified to the defendant's possession of the still and to acts of the defendant which tended to show that the still was controlled by him—that is, his trying to destroy it. The defendant admitted it was in his house but denied having possession. The defect in admitting the illegally gotten evidence of the defendant's incriminatory acts was not cured. This differs from the case of *Blowe v. State*, 130 Miss. 112, 93 So. 577, because in *Blowe v. State* the defendant took the stand and testified to the possession of the goods, the only fact illegally proven.

The officers under authority of a search warrant searched the premises of the defendant and found Jamaca Ginger, wine, and empty bottles, all of which they testified to. The defendant admitted everything to which the officers testified. Therefore, it was immaterial whether the search warrant was good or not. *Prine v. State*, 158 Miss. 435, 130 So. 687. Even if the defendant has objected to the admission of the illegal evidence, if he later testifies to the facts illegally admitted, the error is corrected. *Blowe v. State*, 130 Miss. 112, 93 So. 577.

NELSON CAUTHEN.

BOOK REVIEWS

CASES AND MATERIALS ON TRUSTS AND ESTATES. Vol. I, Property Series. By Richard R. Powell. St. Paul: West Publishing Company, 1932. pp. xliii, 1027.

Much has been said but not a great deal done in recent years about a reclassification of legal subject matter from the standpoint of relation and function, evincing a desire to get away from the fallacious abstractions incident to divisions by definition of principles through a reduction of logical relationships to terms—whereby the good lawyer with a *legal grasp* is expected to bring his adversary to the same fateful end!

It may be unfortunate that the American Law Institute began operations at a time when the functional idea was beginning to take shape and expression,[1] or perhaps it were better to say that it is unfortunate that there are many who think the two must *necessarily* constitute rival schools of thought and that cleaving to the one we must forsake all others.

It is believed that Professor Powell's organization is a successful demonstration of the valuable features of conceptualism and realism with a balanced emphasis on each, i. e. enough of history and concept to gain perspective and explanation, sufficient of function and its relation to human activity to promote a better sense of proportion and application.[2]

The first volume of a series of three which have for their object the replacement of the traditional courses in Trusts, Future Interests and Wills, it would seem that the editor's assumption of the "inseparability of the interacting factors" of these is quite valid. There can be no doubt of the added efficiency in reducing duplication and classroom hours. But aside from this economy, many teachers (of trusts particularly perhaps) will welcome the replacement of the "time-consuming teaching vehicle of the earlier English cases"[3] by a concise, well-written introduction to the English historical background in textual form for the three concepts and the entire absence of attempted fundamental distinctions, e. g. between a trust and a bailment, a tort, a debt, etc., rendered unnecessary by the method of approach, so that in case "A delivers to B the possession of his horse which he directs B to keep in

---

1 "The danger is that law schools and writers may in the future follow the more logical arrangement of Prof. Richard Powell of Columbia, leaving the law of trusts to suffer the fate of a poorly arranged index to case material. Until that time comes, however, it seems inevitable that the American Law Institute follow the classifications with which most courts and lawyers are familiar . . . ."—Arnold, Restatement of the Law of Trusts, 31 Col. L. Rev. 800, 802.

2 "The unreality resulting from attempting to divide up the law into small parts, each dogmatically stated apart from all other rules and apart from its actual operation in modern society, is illustrated in a critique of the Restatement of Trusts by Professor T. W. Arnold."—Clark, Restatement of Contracts, 42 Yale L. J. 659.

But see Scott, Restatement of the Law of Trusts, 31 Col. L. R. 1266.

3 Gulliver, Review of Scott's Select Cases and Other Authorities on the Law of Trusts, 51 Yale L. J. 786, 787.

his stable, we (are not required to) simply observe the transaction, look at
A and B and at the horse in the stable, and say to ourselves, 'It is evident that
in the absence of a contrary intention no trust has arisen here' '' and then
pass on to the next distinction.4

Of primary interest will be the practical innovation of correlating law
with this living age in a chapter on ''some material facts and trends in current
American life'' for informational purposes as a predicate to the methods now
functioning for the distribution of wealth which determine the plan of organization of the book. The remainder of the introductory matter, which begins the case form, delineates conceptually trusts, future interests, and inter
vivos transactions which have post mortem operation. The second part of the
book treats the formal rules for ascertaining the manifestly desired disposition
of property in relation to these conceptual devices, while the third and last
part presents primarily the building of an instrument which will accurately
manifest the desires of the disposer.

Added attractive features of the book are the insertion of questions after
the cases as a time saver in advance acquaintanceship of the student with the
related problems suggested, and the summarization of law review articles and
cases in foot-notes instead of the usual bare citations.

R. J. FARLEY.

CONVICTING THE INNOCENT. ERRORS OF CRIMINAL JUSTICE. By
    Edwin M. Borchard. Publication of the Institute of Human Relations.
    New Haven: Yale University Press, 1932. pp. xxix, 421.

Professor Borchard has selected from twenty-six states and the District
of Columbia sixty-two cases, and from England three cases, of convictions of
persons whose innocence was later established.

Each case is related in an interesting narrative, giving the circumstances
of the crime, the entanglement of the convicted person, a summary of the
evidence, the prejudices, and the discovery of the truth. Each case is verified,
and the court records, interviews of officials, etc., are cited.

An interpretation of the cases points to the following causes as set out
in the Introductory Chapter: (1) Mistaken identification: often by the victim
of the crime violence. (2) Circumstantial evidence leading to wrong conclusions. (3) Perjury. (4) Carelessness and incompetence of the prosecution;
also overzealousness of the prosecutor because of desire of prestige with the
public. (5) Zealousness of the police or detectives; and negligence in over-
looking or even suppressing evidence. (6) Use of prior convictions as evidence
to prejudice jury. (7) Public impatience with the escape of so many guilty
persons. (8) Confessions obtained by ''third degree'' methods. (9) Lack of
funds of the accused to obtain proper counsel and evidence. (10) Lack of
power of the appellate court to review facts as well as law.

Solutions are offered to some of the causes: statutory changes would
eliminate part; others demand a higher level of intelligence or state of mind
in selecting public officers. Some of these causes have no remedy. ''Finally,
if, in spite of these practical precautions against error, an innocent man is
convicted of crime, and it is later established that he had no connection with it,
the least that the State can do to vindicate itself and make restitution to the

---

4 Arnold, *op cit.* Page 804. Brackets mine.

innocent victim is to grant him an indemnity, not as a matter of grace and favor but as a matter of right.''

The author does not pretend that the cases show that a great percentage of those convicted are innocent, but seeks to impress the public with the seriousness of any one case and to arouse interest in restitution and remuneration for victims. ''The State must necessarily prosecute persons legitimately suspected of crime; but when it is discovered after conviction that the wrong man was condemned, the least the State can do to right this essentially irreparable injury is to reimburse the innocent victim, by an appropriate indemnity for the loss and damage suffered.''

A history of the developments in providing for State indemnity is reviewed, showing the present status of the law in Europe and the United States with proposals to the existing legislatures.

EVERETT E. COOK.